T0319140

Cambridge Elements ≡

Elements in Twenty-First Century Music Practice
edited by
Simon Zagorski-Thomas
London College of Music, University of West London

REIMAGINE TO REVITALISE

New Approaches to Performance Practices Across Cultures

Charulatha Mani
School of Music
The University of Queensland

CAMBRIDGE
UNIVERSITY PRESS

CAMBRIDGE
UNIVERSITY PRESS

University Printing House, Cambridge CB2 8BS, United Kingdom

One Liberty Plaza, 20th Floor, New York, NY 10006, USA

477 Williamstown Road, Port Melbourne, VIC 3207, Australia

314–321, 3rd Floor, Plot 3, Splendor Forum, Jasola District Centre,
New Delhi – 110025, India

103 Penang Road, #05–06/07, Visioncrest Commercial, Singapore 238467

Cambridge University Press is part of the University of Cambridge.

It furthers the University's mission by disseminating knowledge in the pursuit of
education, learning, and research at the highest international levels of excellence.

www.cambridge.org
Information on this title: www.cambridge.org/9781108829731
DOI: 10.1017/9781108903905

First published 2021

A catalogue record for this publication is available from the British Library.

ISBN 978-1-108-82973-1 Paperback
ISSN 2633-4585 (online)
ISSN 2633-4577 (print)

Cambridge University Press has no responsibility for the persistence or accuracy of
URLs for external or third-party internet websites referred to in this publication
and does not guarantee that any content on such websites is, or will remain,
accurate or appropriate.

Reimagine to Revitalise

New Approaches to Performance Practices Across Cultures

Elements in Twenty-First Century Music Practice

DOI: 10.1017/9781108903905
First published online: July 2021

Charulatha Mani
School of Music, The University of Queensland

Author for correspondence: Charulatha Mani, c.mani@uq.edu.au

Abstract: This Element links intercultural musical understanding in the present to the reconsideration of the history of Western music from a global perspective. It examines the compositional style of composer Claudio Monteverdi from the perspective of Karnatik music of South India through the complementary methodological lenses of historical and comparative musicology and features a critical analysis of vocal ornamentation and technique, using theory and artistic research. The outcomes include an innovative approach to studying musics from the past, a decahedral framework of hybridity between early opera and Karnatik music, and practice-based vocal enactments of hybridity, as both process and artistic product of the plurality. The research design harks back to a historical time in early modern Europe, wherein a borderless mobility of musicians from the East paved the way to an unprecedented plurality of musical cultures, and holds deep implications for diversity in and decolonisation of current music performance and education.

Keywords: Karnatik, Monteverdi, culture, Gorgie, voice

ISBNs: 9781108829731 (PB), 9781108903905 (OC)
ISSNs: 2633-4585 (online), 2633-4577 (print)

Contents

1 The Pressing Need: An Interrogation of Practices

What we believe to be the sound of early opera today is, in all probability, very different from what it was some 400 years ago. We do not know how their voices sounded or how exactly they may have delivered ornamentations. We know from the notations and historical evidence that they sang with great virtuosity and that there was a culture of profuse ornamentation and improvisation. The ways of approaching the uncertainties in how early opera sounded present an exciting opportunity for research from a musicological and historical perspective. Further, early modern Europe was a centre for great mobility with travellers from the East bringing with them not only tangible artefacts and musical instruments but also intangible cultural heritage. In light of this cultural complexity at the time, exploring early opera through the lens of the music of a cultural other, not least from the East, becomes a promising and rewarding enterprise.

As a primary part of my recently completed doctoral research, I explored the musical declamation style of Italian composer Claudio Monteverdi in relation to a comparable sung-speech style of spontaneous exposition of poetry in Karnatik music of South India, the *Viruttam*. I explored Monteverdi's writing for voice in *L'Orfeo* (1607), widely considered to be the first operatic masterpiece ever written, using the vocal style typical of Karnatik music (Mani, 2019a). The research adopted historical and comparative musicology, and artistic research as its methods. My position as a Karnatik vocal performer from Chennai, India, with over two decades of performance and teaching experience in traditional and intercultural contexts, served as a suitable vantage point for this research. My transition to becoming a composer and intercultural performer in my current home of four years, Brisbane, Australia, was also embedded in the inquiry.

As a migrant woman from postcolonial India to a settler colonial state, I found myself seeking ways to disinvest from colonially conferred modes of being, knowing, and performing, and a peek into a culturally diverse historical time in Western music offered me a window of opportunity to do so through music. It was at the interstices of the musico-poetic and performative, in both Karnatik and early operatic singing styles, that I positioned my work as *interrogative artistic research in music* (Mani, 2020b). This methodology model ensured that the creative processes that framed the research triggered reflections not only on the divergent musical materials, tools, and techniques, but also on the dominant narratives that have come to frame the beliefs and identities of the performance cultures at interplay.

Much scholarship has demonstrated the intersections of historically informed performance practices and artistic research, particularly in the context of

Monteverdi's early operas (Davidson, 2015, 2016; Kaleva, 2014; Lawrence-King, 2014). Davidson describes the role of historical knowledge in creating her production of *L'Orfeo, Monteverdi Reclaimed*:

> With their own interpretations of period treatises on music and rhetoric, the members of the production team (including myself) acted as the possessors of historical knowledge during rehearsals. Our job was to translate this knowledge into a meaningful experience for the performers and explore practical means for the performance company to acquire this historical knowledge. (Davidson, 2015, p. 102)

I notice that she clearly demarcates between roles here; the production team are designated as possessors of historical knowledge, and performers are designated as receivers and processors of this 'translated' knowledge as experience. Artist-researchers, however, can acquire knowledge from theory *and* experience it in practice, thereby becoming active agents in such 'translation', bridging the cognitive and the subjective. They can, through interrogation of the theories of such knowledges and the assumptions therein, also become agents of disruption, catalysis, and change. Whitney's (2015) definition of practice-based research speaks to these ideas and takes me back to the issue at hand, namely, methods that look to musicology as the first port of call: '[Practice-based research is] research developed and led by professional musicians as principal researchers on some aspect of their professional practice that involves their own performance as an integral part of the investigation' (p. 93).

When one's own practice becomes central to an investigation, and informants from musicology and history become companions to such an investigation, insights and impact can flow from the personal to the public; from the self-centric to a sociocultural and even political paradigm. In a time when ways of being and knowing across music performance and education are being reconsidered with the aim of 'decolonising' practices, it is worthwhile to unpack the colonised state of the canonical, even in master narratives that surround Western art music. The freedom to *choose* elements from music of the past and bring these selections into their interpretation in the present, one might argue, lies with the performer. However, for fear of being sidelined from the centre to the margins, performers are still waiting in the wings; still looking for permission – perhaps from proxy gatekeepers to dead composers, from a certain rung of society to which they feel beholden, or even from their institutions. Sometimes the hardest thing to do is to give oneself permission to step out of the boundaries into newness. Interrogative artistic research affords such an opportunity within the safety net of academia. Choosing what to bring, and how to bring it into contemporary contexts, when undertaken from such a position, might be a gentler way for those living within the confines of convention to hurdle into the contentious zone of non-conformance. Such an act is a signifier of respect for the past, a critical evaluation of historical evidence, 'independent thinking', 'positivistic enthusiasm', and an openness to possibilities in the present, as Taruskin (1995, p. 5) argued a few decades ago.

Today, there is a pressing need to reconsider the history of Western music from a global perspective, not least to contextualise and critically appraise its cultural and ethical complexities in the light of the current superdiverse societies that we, as music practitioners and audiences, currently inhabit (Westerlund, 2019). From the perspective of a coloured woman's living and working in academia in a Western country, musical hybridity, I advance, is not only enacted in the liminal spaces between diverse cultures and their musics as we understand them today, but also in the ever-changing space between history and the present: our histories and our present; our overt cultures and those of others, as enacted in the complexity of the present. Musical cultures which are perceived as overtly disjointed today may have had a lot in common in history as, for instance, Irving's (2010) groundbreaking work on globally considered history of Western music establishes.

Many performance practices across cultures that are currently revered as 'traditional' are edifices of convention that have been constructed over the years in response to a wide and complex gamut of sociocultural parameters. For instance, the Karnatik music tradition emerged from a nationalist, politically driven, systematic decimation of the embodied practices of hereditary female temple performer-courtesans, the *devadasis* (Soneji, 2011; L. Subramanian, 2006). Ethically, then, Karnatik music is a form that has been appropriated; culturally, however, it is now the single most powerful representative of the classical music of Southern India to the world (Krishna, 2013, 2018). We continue to confront this paradox as long shadows of the past relentlessly taunt the apparent neoliberalist growth trend in Karnatik performance culture. The *#MeToo* movement in Karnatik music is an example. It brought forth the distraught voices of many female music students and performers who were taken advantage of and exploited by powerful male performers, organisers, and *guru(s)*. No doubt the *guru(s)* who behaved in such a deplorable way were celebrated within the performance culture and beyond for their allegiance to conventional approaches – from how a piece of music should be sung to how a (female) performer must dress, look, gesture, and sound. However, perpetuating a performance culture of supplication and adherence to misappropriated notions of convention may be tantamount to fettering oneself to the implicit power structures of patriarchy and the hegemony of master narratives. When we strive to sustain practices from history, I call for a critical and ethical approach.

Today, we live in an age of distributed creativity and collaborative interactivity: between people, cultures, machines, and ecosystems (e.g. Haraway, 2004). In such an age, to be true to an artistic work that has been handed down to us in unbroken succession through history is not so much to fetishise the murky details that surround it as it is to regard it with fresh co-creative eyes – with eyes that have contended with the complexities of the present and are ready for romanticising the past, even if it might just be a means of escape into a fleeting moment of fantasy with history as a co-conspirator. It calls for a spirit of adventure that could enter into an interpretive dance with the work rather than a passive and wary 'gazing'. In a way, such an approach to music from the past answers Leech-Wilkinson's (2017, para. 2) recent provocation: '[S]cores can generate powerful experiences not just in ways that are taught, heard, recorded and approved now, but in imaginably and unimaginably different ways. So why are they not allowed to?'

Whether the work is a composition of Karnatik composer Thyagaraja (handed down orally) or the operatic work of Claudio Monteverdi (handed down and interpreted over time as and using versions of the score), as practitioners dealing with these materials in our creative spheres of enterprise, we have a right to *responsibly* reinterpret them. Such interpretation needs to occur in a manner that is nurturing to the work, in a way that compels the artist and audiences to spend more time with the work, in a way that ensures participative enjoyment of every beautiful detail and that results in the making of a bespoke co-created version of it. The values and judgements ascribed to rightful and aesthetic interpretations of works from the past are contentious at best. However, subjectivity comes to one's rescue in such cases; a rightful interpretation could be engendered through minimal improvisation or with pronounced departures. It could involve newer approaches to performing established material or steer established approaches into unknown terrain. It could thwart the established every step of the way, yet, it could be meaningful for the present.

For instance, a female Karnatik performer, who is currently actively discouraged from gesturing and moving on stage could sidestep convention and stand up for her rights. She could express herself corporeally as she sings. While this is indeed a blatant disregard of *convention*, it is a welcome interrogation of all that had historically shamed the performing female body in Karnatik music through an embracing not only of the corporeal, but also of the perished *devadasi* tradition of singing and dancing (Soneji, 2011). I make this point also to highlight the important distinction between convention and tradition. Convention has overtones of imposition and compulsion; tradition on the other hand has always been understood as dynamic, responsive to sociocultural factors, and grounded in historical fact (Mani, 2020a). The seated position, conventional in current Karnatik performance practice, is quite the opposite of tradition. The *devadasis* historically danced while singing, and continued this practice over centuries at least, until they were forced to abandon their traditional form of practice in the wake of the Karnatik music reform of the early twentieth century. Their embodied manner of presentation is the 'true' Karnatik tradition or norm, but has been lost to us due to social injustices against the community in the wake of the nationalist movement in India (L. Subramanian, 2006). This loss of tradition is lamentable, as it has stripped any element of drama or emotion from the performance practice of Karnatik music of today; an example of tradition losing to the politics of convention, much to the detriment of the artform. As Leech-Wilkinson (2017, para. 8) notes in the context of Western art music: 'There is artistry in promoting convention, no doubt, but it is art without originality. It reassures, it does not challenge. Is that what we want from art? Doesn't art involve offering new ways to see aspects of ourselves, not old ways of reassuring ourselves that all is well?'

This provocation from Leech-Wilkinson is entirely valid and remains central to my inquiry. Old ways that reassure us that all is well are servants of convention and therefore the nemesis of the critical dismantling of those aspects of convention that may be untenable, whether artistically or ethically. Permission to cohabit with a work can come wholeheartedly only from within the performer's being. Giving ourselves permission to live with a slice of musical history through keeping alive the key performative quality of creative impulse rather than reverence, in a way, anthropomorphises the work and imbues it with human qualities. We respond warmly to these qualities, we conspire with them, we 'become' them, and we co-opt them into newer zones of play (Davidson & Correia, 2001).

As the world changes, so must convention; so must ways of knowing and expressing music such that it enfranchises the traditional but disengages with the inappropriate or impractical. If performance is to be accepted as a 'primary mode of signification', as Cook (2015, p. 14) advocates, and not text, it must be that singular tool that connects us to our immediacy in this world and become an ontological locus of investigation, from the ground up. If this ideal informs our reclaiming of work from the past as in and for the present, that could offer one rightful way to disinvest in the canon.

Further, strategising for and staging performance are both dovetailed acts and magic wands that performer/curators wave at the world to interrogate it or shock it, as they deem necessary. It is in response to the sociocultural stimuli around us that we reconfigure lived performance practice and epistemologies that propagate such practice into the future. Therefore, originality, creativity, and sociocultural interrogation together have the power to reinvigorate performance practices of the past in the present from the grass-root levels across both theory and practice, that is, from musicological analysis to artistic research and through to performance. Preparing work *for* performance could then be historically inspired, historically romanticised, historically pluralised, and historically interrogated. These complementary positions are tropes to approaching historically informed performance without burden or guilt – just the way it ought to be, here and now.

The notion of altering the aesthetic of a certain musical form – whether the Karnatik musico-poetic form, *Viruttam*, or Monteverdian declamation – using elements from another, entails a shift in the identity of the form as well as in the identity of the artist engaged in such a blending.[1]. This concomitancy in 'shifts' is one method to ensure that we invest ourselves holistically into those new ways to approach art, ways that we seek. The performer and work transitioning into the new, in tandem, also brings to the fore the differences between musical forms, cultures, and compliance models as much as it does the similarities. The sites of convergences and divergences systematically enable a brewing of frameworks of interrogation. Crispin's (2015) notes that new approaches to composition in Western art music, such as co-creativity, serve to interrogate identity of established forms by challenging composer hegemony and narrowing the gulf between the composer and performer: 'The hermetically-sealed nature of these claims [of compositional hegemony] is increasingly being challenged, not least by the incursion of improvisational and co-creative practices into the arena of composition' (Crispin, 2015, p. 319).

The question of the ontology of a historical work of art has been debated over decades in the field (e.g., Goodman, 1976, pp. 113–121) and particularly in opera (e.g., Abbate, 2004; Calcagno, 2012, pp. 17–20). The overall text-versus-act debate in Western art music has resulted in the emergence of criticisms of *werktreue*, *texttreue*, and text-fetishism (Goehr, 1992; Taruskin, 1995). In parallel, however, the question of what convention is and how it links to or deviates from tradition in Karnatik performance practice is an under-researched area (Krishna, 2013, pp. 9–15). In opera, tensions arise at the interstices of text-work-act, and in Karnatik at the interstices of prescribed convention and the freedom of self-representation. It is at these interstitial zones of tension that hybrid practices could reinvigorate through an active reimagination of practices of the past. Haynes's (2007) comment, 'when you say something differently, you say something different', (p. 19) strikes a chord with my current research towards hybridising Karnatik elements and early opera.

---

[1] Viruttam is an exposition of Tamil poetry in Karnatik raga and is delivered without rhythmic cycles. The poetic metre dictates the time in this form. The Viruttam form is expressive of poetic emotion. To learn more about the Viruttam, see Krishna (2013); Mani (2019a).

An attempt at hybridity of musical practices needs ideally to be evaluated from dual perspectives, in this case, Karnatik and early operatic. This research comes at a time when there is an ongoing movement in Western scholarship advocating for newer approaches to musics from the past. The tropes of subjectivity, co-creativity, and artistic research are emerging as powerful, complementary lenses to draw out such approaches through artmaking (e.g., Cook, 2018; Leech-Wilkinson & Prior, 2014; Östersjö, 2017). This study also comes at a time in Monteverdian scholarship when the constructions of meaning in Monteverdi's operas are being problematised from several new musicological angles (Cusick, 2007, pp. 249–260). Approaches such as new historicism (considering original historical concerns; e.g., Carter, 2002; Tomlinson 1981); new criticism (reading the poetry sans context; see Tomlinson, 1987); feminist critique (e.g., Cusick, 1994; Gordon, 2004; Heller, 2003, 2014; MacNeil, 2003; McClary, 1991); and historically informed performance practice (e.g., Calcagno, 2002, 2012; Schneider, 2012; Wistreich, 1994, 2013) are only a few of the various lenses that scholars have adopted, from the 1990s through to the present, in examining Monteverdi's musical choices, and the implications for research and performance in the present.

Further ways to contextualise Monteverdi's musical and semantic paradigms came forth in Monteverdi's 450th year commemorative conferences hosted at Mantua, Cremona, and Venice, which I was fortunate to attend (Monteverdi Festival, 2017). One of the issues that emerged through these conferences as under-researched in Monteverdian studies was the role of historical vocal technique in Monteverdi's operas. The fact that we have little knowledge of how the pre-romantic voice sounded needs ideally be an incentive to exploring newer possibilities of addressing this vocal style. Instead, in early music vocal performance and pedagogy, there is a fossilised approach to the typical historical voice of the seventeenth century. As Leech-Wilkinson (2017) provokes: 'When only the most brilliantly obedient can succeed, we have a serious problem with underlying beliefs about what music should be' (para. 11). Importantly, a global reconstruction of the history of Western music is a recently burgeoning field of scholarship that is intertwined with practical attempts to interrogate normative soundings of canonised music. An example of an initiative of great impact in that line of investigation is the *Balzan Project* of Reinhardt Strohm (2018), on which I shall expand a little later.

Overall, this study looks to interpret Monteverdi from a Karnatik musical perspective as much as it looks to interpret the musico-poetic form in Karnatik music from Monteverdi's 'musical drama' perspective. It therefore aims to make a significant contribution to the way in which his musical language is currently being interpreted in the West, across its approaches to his musical material as raga, his continuo as raga-based chords, and his ornamentation as *gamaka*. Monteverdi's music has been termed transitional, situated at the precipice of the Renaissance, heralding the Baroque (Chafe, 1992, pp. 1–20). Monteverdi's music has been exhaustively examined from modal hexachordal perspectives and from a tonality approach (e.g., Chafe, 1992; Chew, 1989; McClary, 2004; Rosand, 2007, pp. 346–373), to name but a few models of analysis. Despite such in-depth approaches, recent scholars have called for 'a more intensive discussion of tonal concepts of the period' (Schulze, 2010, p. 105). In line with Schulze (2010), I adopt a research approach that both musicologically and practically engages with the Monteverdian melodic sphere. This hitherto unexplored perspective could be one way through which fresh insights on his music, across tonal concepts to dramatic devices, might emerge. The domain of academic research presents the ideal ground for practice-based knowledge to interact with theory, analysis, and method, thus rendering such insights analysable and transferrable. Keith Powers (2018), based on a recent interview with noted period performers of the Boston Early Music Festival, observes: 'From Monteverdi to Mozart, the notion of period performance – or historically informed performance – has grown up. And all music, not just Renaissance and Baroque compositions, can benefit from the newfound adulthood' (K. Powers, 2018, para. 3).

In the West, scholars and performers are calling for such 'newfound adulthood' across canonical works, primarily from a performance angle. This research begins from ground-up musicological analysis and builds up to practice, rendering the notion of being historically informed as lying beyond the realms of performance, and into the realm of context, content, form, materials, techniques, and tools. On the one hand, with their 'symbolic poverty' (Cook, 2007, pp. 301–305), the scores of the baroque, in general, enrich the scope for performers' creativity; on the other, they are a subtle indicator that historical informants for music of the baroque often lie within factors extraneous to the score, such as the sociopolitical circumstances that led to a certain style, the cultures at interplay at the point of genesis of a work, and the social settings that underscored the work. A study of these can contextualise the work better in the present, allowing for interpretive freedom. Lutenist and Monteverdi specialist Stephen Stubbs responds to K. Powers: 'after 50 years of performing Monteverdi ... rather than "historically informed performance" why don't we just go with "informed performance"?' (K. Powers, 2018, para. 23). The adumbration of Monteverdi's aesthetic into the Karnatik declamatory style, and the interweaving of Karnatik raga and ornament into the Monteverdian dramatic fabric, is an exemplar of an 'informed performance' that looks to style, aesthetic, and inherent cultural divergences as a cogent whole. For instance, in

Mani (2019b), I have demonstrated that ways to approach Monteverdian ornamentation can be effectively communicated to students of Western opera using a comparable South Indian ornamentation technique.

The cultural plurality in early modern Europe during Monteverdi's time is the striking feature that finds itself under-represented in the so-called authentic attempts at portraying Monteverdi today. Theory and practice pertaining to a global reconsideration of the history of Western music will greatly benefit from the histories of cultural mobility and their manifestations in and as musical practice in the present. There is a considerable evidence base that Italy in the sixteenth and seventeenth centuries was the playground of cultural diversity and richness, abounding in travellers, exotic instruments, and art. Today, many parts of the world are experiencing a comparable heterogeneity and even super-diversity – in cultures, musics, and art. If there is one feature that we would do well to preserve in what we believe is historically informed performance of Monteverdi today, it would be the underscoring ethos of plurality – of styles, of voices, of ways to approach the melodic material, of ways to improvise and ornament, and of ways to emote. Overall, an ethos of creativity and originality that is unfettered by the norms that were erected in the romantic period and after.

The British early music movement somewhat achieved this ethos. Nick Wilson writes about his opera debut in the 1990s: It was 'far removed' from 'authentic performance', he notes.

> My famous Act III recitative *Possente spirto,* for example, was sung not to the echoes of cornetts, sackbuts, and harps, as originally scored, but to the distinctively 20th-century accompaniment of a pair of saxophones and a bank of synthesizers. Nevertheless, we *were* performing Monteverdi's opera, and we *were* deeply committed to making it work for our audience. (Wilson, 2013, p.ix)

Engendering lived sensorial experiences of sound and sight for the audience, when considered the primary duty of a performer, supersedes allegiances to score or any style. Further, Cook (2015, p. 15) has noted: 'HIP [historically informed performance] was and is based on an iterative method in which knowledge flows in both directions between musicologists and performers', clarifying his stance that historically informed performance (HIP) is an *ongoing* exchange between the performances that shaped history, and history that is being made through performance, all in the presence of an audience that partakes of the enacted sentiment. This is particularly significant in the case of a work such as *L'Orfeo*, which was introduced first as performance and only later as text (Calcagno, 2012). Knowledge is continually constructed through each performance. A performance of a work that is approached 'with an open mind, and open ears to hear beyond the current performances of it' is one that merits pride of place in performance practice (Doğantan-Dack, 2015, p. 36). Such an approach to works from history aligns with the sociocultural state of the present, the musicians' mental state in the present, and the relevance of cultural plurality in the present.

In this Element, I draw on a slice of my exploration of *L'Orfeo* from a Karnatik perspective and demonstrate alliances between musicology and performance, between history and imagination, and between musical materials, techniques, and tools across two musical cultures that *seem* oceans apart. The key to starting a practical dialogue with Monteverdi's music, for me, lay in analysing and interpreting his ornamentation style through my culturally contingent Karnatik vocal practice that is indeed driven by ornamentation. Referred to as *alankara* (the bejewelled) in the *Natyasastra* (historical treatise of performing arts of India, circa 2 CE), ornamentation has been and continues to be regarded as the most distinctive sonic quality that Indian music possesses (Kassebaum, 2000). Monteverdi's Act III declamation from *L'Orfeo*, *Possente Spirto* was highly suitable for examining the nature, functions, and semantic connotations of vocal ornamentation, and through them the multiple facets of the musical style.

The piece is a stellar exemplar of the seventeenth-century embellished monody for the virtuosic voice, and is contextualised in drama, rendering it a powerful tool for storytelling. The ornate passagework that marks this piece (*ornatus*) rhetorically communicates in a way that delights the listener (*delectare*), rather than move them (*movere*) (Schwindt, 2014, pp. 240–241; Steinheuer, 2007, p. 139). Semantically, Monteverdi uses ornamentation in *Possente Spirto* to establish an interesting nexus between the context of Orfeo pleading with the boatman, Caronte, the characterisation of Orfeo as a virtuosic singer, and the intent of the drama at this point – to render the Orphic plea rhetorically unconvincing. The ornamentation does not move the listener, it only delights them. *Possente Spirto* therefore lends itself to consideration on multiple levels – across rhetorical intent to ornamental grandeur.

As a vocal performer, it was *Possente Spirto*'s embellished framework that attracted me to Monteverdi's music in the first place. Therefore, to systematically erect the framework of hybridity between Karnatik music and the Monteverdian musical style, I shift my gaze to a different time and place in history, where a battle between word and melody yielded a new genre that enfolded emotion, drama, and rhetoric into a spectacular whole – opera. Rhetoric, emotion (*bhava*), and ornamentation are key considerations in Karnatik music too, rendering them useful registers of interrogation of cultural histories and practices using theory and practice.

Accordingly, Sections 2 and 3 of this Element examine Monteverdi's declamatory style from an intercultural perspective, offering a globally positioned framework into the essentially Eurocentric world of early music. I propose a *decahedral framework of hybridity* between Karnatik musico-poetic forms and Monteverdian declamation as a methodology model to illustrate how a ground-up approach to an interrogation of performance cultures may be evidenced from an intercultural angle. Section 4 of the Element draws on a single dimension of interaction from the decahedron: ornamentation. I leverage musicological research that reveals uncanny similarities in ornamentation between the two styles to present the viability of an intercultural reimagination of the oft-romanticised early modern cultural plurality in the present. Section 5 addresses the issue of the need for a global reconsideration of the history of Western music in the light of the analyses and framework proposed, histories of cultural mobility, and the current rallying from artistic and performance researchers for newer approaches to the established.

2 Understanding Monteverdi's Poetic Aesthetic

In the first decade of the seventeenth century, a musical language that held the need to convey dramatic meaning as its primary responsibility was developed in Italy. A sequence of events would bring into focus a composer, who, in defending his unique signatory compositional blend of word and melody, would mark the arrival of a mature musical syntax that could convey poetry, emotion, virtuosic grandeur, and drama, all at once. It would be a style known for its musical 'imitation of word' and would admirably address the humanist need for 'representation of [human] emotion' in and through musical drama (Rosand, 2011, p. 149). Opera, over the next four centuries, would evolve and establish itself as a powerful, interdisciplinary medium of musical expression. It is through this universal lens of emotion and human vocal expression that I frame my approach to hybridity.

Composer Claudio Monteverdi, referred to by many as 'the creator of modern music' (Schrade, 1950) was not alone in his journey in crafting the genre of opera; nor was his musical idiom without historical precedent or continuity. The trajectory of development of opera at the time was closely aligned to the dynamic changes in the prevailing performance cultures, particularly in relation to the solo voice and its potential to communicate to audiences. A historically grounded discussion on the genesis of musical declamation is warranted here, before attempting to cohabit Monteverdi's musical world.

Revisiting the Ways of the Ancients

> I would rather be moderately praised for the new style than greatly praised for the ordinary.
>
> (Monteverdi, *lettera* dated 23 October 1633 in Stevens, 1985, p. 85)

To claim that the origins of opera were inspired by the quest for finding expressivity through a solo voice would not be an exaggeration when claimed in the light of an examination of the unique ways of composition that emerged in early seventeenth-century Italy. Poetry became 'destined to *audiences*' during that period rather than merely to readers and this was made possible through music (Calcagno, 2002, p. 384).

Gary Tomlinson (1987), Claude Palisca (1985, 1989), and Barbara Russano Hanning (1980) present a few of the most authoritative accounts of the transformation of musical ideals from the Renaissance to what is regarded as early opera, around the first half of the seventeenth century, during which time Monteverdi's operas would first unfold across Mantua and Venice. Their scholarly discussions centre on a series of events that led to music being regarded as an artform that could hold tremendous sway over the affective qualities in humans. The Aristotelian school of thought regarded music as art, meant for the senses (Palisca, 1985, p. 21). Accordingly, music and drama were deemed forms of *mimesis*; they imitated human feelings: 'When men hear imitations in music, their feelings move in sympathy' (Aristotle, 2014, p. 2126). Feelings began to be understood in the sixteenth century as being manifest through music, and this awareness was linked to the beliefs of humanism that were burgeoning across artistic disciplines during the time.

Early humanists of the sixteenth century were interested in the Greek tragedies. These, they incorrectly believed, were dramatic forms that were sung throughout (Fabbri, 1994, p. 97–98; Palisca, 1985). As the *Documentary Studies and Translations* of Palisca (1989, pp. 13–20) demonstrate, humanist knowledge was theoretical, and acquired primarily from the writings of Aristotle (*Problems, Poetics, Politics*), Plato (*The Republic; Laws*), Ptolemy (*Harmonics*), Aristides Quintilianus (*De Musica*), and others. The music of ancient Greece, being an oral tradition, furnished very few examples of actual notation. Through a consolidated understanding of theory, however, the humanists began to forge practical approaches to imagining Greek sung-tragedies, as drama, in their present.

The desire to emulate the ancients in music-making gained momentum due to the efforts of a patron of the arts, Count Giovanni Bardi. Bardi regularly convened a group, the Florentine Camerata. The Camerata met between 1576 and 1582 at Bardi's home in Florence, and became the agency that led forward the inquiry into ancient sources in the second half of the sixteenth century (Palisca, 1989; Pirrotta & Fortune, 1954, pp. 169–189). As Palisca (1989, pp. 84–85) construes, 'Bardi wanted to see music return to its ancient function of seconding poetry and moving listeners to various passions.' The backdrop of the humanist agenda of the revival of antiquity became an active arena to foreground and forge a text-driven and delivery-oriented culture in then-contemporary composition. They were leveraging history to break with convention and were essentially forging a new approach to composing with and for text, which would become a formidable tradition in the coming centuries.

The Camerata operated on the premise that Greek drama was delivered in a song-like manner, though, not as a song (Hanning, 1980, pp. 3–12), and this speech-song dichotomy gave rise to the unique genre of declamation. Cultural historian Ruth Katz (1994, p. 56) identifies 'declamation' as 'song-like speech', indicating that the creation of declamation was predicated on an intended style of delivery, rather than as a mere compositional variant to song, rendering such a style arguably performance-derived. Musicians and scholars of the time, including singer/composer and organist Jacopo Peri, virtuoso singer/composer Giulio Caccini, poet/librettist Rinuccini, aristocrat/composer Emilio Cavalieri, researcher Vincenzo Galilei, and aristocrat Jacopo Corsi belonged to the Camerata, which Grout and Williams (2003, pp. 34–36) refer to as an 'informal academy', and Katz (1994, p. 49) as an 'invisible college'.

As is arguably the case in much artistic research, the Camerata's impetus for re-creation of the ancient stemmed from a problem that they perceived in the music of their prevailing practice. Renaissance polyphony models, they believed, obfuscated the words. If poetry had to be conveyed as drama and listeners to be moved, they decided that a newer model, closer to natural speech, had to be adopted. They directed their research to this end.

Vincenzo Galilei, notably, drew on the work of Florentine researcher and historian Girolamo Mei's study of Greek history of musical drama. Galilei's (1581) treatise *Dialogo della musica antica et della moderna* is based on his correspondences with Mei and discusses ideas on performance of the ancient fables for modern sensibilities. Palisca declares that Mei was the mentor to the Camerata: "Mei aimed from the start to convince his correspondent mainly of two things: that the music of the Greeks had always been monodic and that only by virtue of this had it been capable of so many marvellous effects (Palisca, 1954, p. 10).

Mei reasons that ancient music was moving because of its monodic nature. Interestingly, Karnatik vocal music is characteristically monodic. I construe that the characteristics of monody and vocal ornamentation are the fundamental points of resonance that could weave together emotion and vocal expression in the context of hybridity between Karnatik music and seventeenth century Italian declamation. Grout and Williams (2003, pp. 35–36) summarise the Camerata's three focus areas: emphasis on the role of the solo singer, seeking ways of 'natural' declamation, and the desire to arrive at solutions that use melodic devices to interpret text effectively. This three-way approach resonates clearly with my research objectives.

As Katz (1994, pp. 54–55) notes, the Camerata was both a forum for 'theoretical discussions' as well as a 'workshop' and 'laboratory' for the 'creation and performance' of music. That musicians and thinkers have always been driven by the desire to de-contextualise concepts of the past and re-contextualise them in *their present* is an exemplary case of historically informed, or rather, historically inspired artistic research, even in the 1600s.

Peri's *L'Euridice* (1600): The Birth of *Recitar Cantando*

Declamation as envisaged by the Camerata unfolded in practice across a series of musical dramas in the first few years of the seventeenth century. The expression *'imitar col canto chi parla'* (Solerti, 1904, pp. 43–44), 'imitating in song a person speaking' (trans. Strunk, 1950, p. 374) was used by Jacopo Peri in the preface to his musical drama *L'Euridice* (1600). *Recitar cantando*, a musical language for 'sung-speech', was emblematic of *'imitar col canto chi parla'*, and quickly achieved the status of being the compositional approach of choice for the declamatory genre that would sustain musical drama for the next several decades (Calcagno, 2002, pp. 384–388).

Emilio Cavalieri, in the preface to his *La rappresentatione di anima et di corpo* (1600) was the first to introduce the term *recitar cantando*, sung-speech. From his preface to *La rappresentatione* we get an idea of the functionality of *recitar cantando*: 'this manner of music which he (Cavalieri) has restored may move listeners to different emotions such as pity and joy tears and laughter' (Solerti, 1904, p. 5). According to Steinheuer (2007, p. 121), Cavalieri's approach to *recitar cantando* was *'cosa mezzana'*, 'halfway between sung and spoken recitation'.

A suite of composed contributions for theatre therefore came into existence at the time and used *recitar cantando* as a point of departure: *Dafne* (1598), *libretto* by Rinuccini, set to music by Peri and Corsi; Peri's *L'Euridice* (1600), Caccini's *Euridice* (1600), and Cavalieri's *La Rappresentatione* (1600). Peri's *L'Euridice* (1600) is an exemplar of the sophistication of this style and finds many parallels with the musical and textual organisation of Monteverdi's first musical drama, *L'Orfeo* (1607), as Tomlinson demonstrates with plentiful examples (1987, pp. 131–141).

However, not one, but at least two styles of monody writing developed from within the Camerata, as Pirrotta and Povoledo (1982) extrapolate. The first was indeed the *recitar cantando*, stemming from Peri's approach, in close alignment also with a recitative style of elevated speech, the *stilo recitativo*. If Peri's interest was in bringing the singing closer to speech, Caccini was interested in exploring the art of singing, as 'affective reactions to dramatic situations' (Pirrotta & Povoledo, 1982, p. 252). This was a style of exploring the predominance of text using music as the means. Katz (1994, p. 58) describes it as 'words finding expression in music'. Pirrotta (1984, p. 244), after consideration of Caccini's approach, refers to such a style as *cantar recitando*, spoken song. This second style of declamation was also related to the madrigalist singing styles of the time that showcased ornamented monody, '*cantar di garbo*' (Carter, 2012, p. 7).

Monteverdi's approach to monody in drama aligned with these prevalent styles: sung-speech and spoken-song. He also deployed unique compositional devices from what he referred to as his Second Practice, the *Seconda Prattica*. The Bolognese theorist Giovanni Maria Artusi's criticisms of Monteverdi's polyphonic madrigals incited Monteverdi to reveal to the world his doctrine of the *Seconda Prattica* and its implications for semantic and emotional emphasis in word-setting (Palisca, 1985, p. 127). I now turn to briefly discuss Monteverdi's background and the attributes of his *Seconda Prattica* that were relevant to his monody style.

Monteverdi's Word-Setting and his *Seconda Prattica* (Second Practice)

Born in Cremona in 1567, Monteverdi started his musical tutelage under Marc'Antonio Ingegneri. He acquired mastery of Renaissance polyphonic writing and proficiency in stringed instruments, including the violin and the viola da gamba. It was in 1587 with his *First Book of Madrigals* that he began his journey into the then well-regarded form of secular music. When the sung-speech agenda was taking hold of musical drama, Claudio Monteverdi was emerging as a significant figure in madrigal composition. The eight madrigal books that he published in his lifetime show his evolving style and served as his point of departure for experimentation within and outside the genre. The year 1590 was pivotal in his life; it marked the arrival of his *Second Book of Madrigals* and his departure from Cremona to join the court of Duke Vincenzo Gonzaga as a string player at Mantua, where he would continue as *maestro di capella* until 1612 enacting some major musical revolutions (Ringer, 2006, pp. 1–19).

Madrigals constitute secular poetry set to polyphony, *usually* according to rules of counterpoint, but not always. Monteverdi's approach and argument would demonstrate and rationalise this point, adopting text-setting as the arbiter at times above purely musical relationships.

Monteverdi was well-versed in the *Prima Prattica* (First Practice) that Gioseffe Zarlino (1558/1968) successfully instilled at the time through his *Istitutioni* (Book 3). The First Practice dealt with the correct usage of consonances, dissonances, and modes. Monteverdi's attitude, however, was additive; he sought a way to improve textual expressivity through his compositions and the First Practice alone did not fulfil this need. Further, as Strunk (1950, p. 302) observes, those were indeed the times when Galilei's *Dialogo* (1581) had been advanced as a 'declaration of war against counterpoint'. This rendered the rules of harmony arguably in opposition to text-centricity – Monteverdi's way of flouting the normative.

A protracted sequence of events that began with vehement criticism of a selection of Monteverdi's madrigals by Artusi led to Monteverdi's declaration of a *Seconda Prattica* with the primary purpose of communicating poetry with the intensity that it deserved. Giovanni Maria Artusi criticised Monteverdi's two madrigals *Cruda Amarilli* and *O Mirtillo*, citing nine examples of departures from convention across them (Palisca, 1985, pp. 127–135). An avowed follower of Zarlino, Artusi was a stickler for the rules of counterpoint. His objections were around Monteverdi's use of dissonances that did not resolve in accordance with the rules. He also complained that Monteverdi did not confine his music to a single modality within a piece; *O Mirtillo,* for instance, begins in one mode and ends in another, depicting the tension between the D-Dorian and G-Mixolydian (McClary, 2004). *Cruda Amarilli* abounds in cadences in the C-plagal, which is different from the mode in which it unfolds, G-authentic (McClary, 2004, pp. 188–192; Palisca, 1985, p. 144–145).

Figures 2.1 and 2.2 show sections from *Cruda Amarilli* to draw attention to a few instances that Artusi found objectionable. In both these instances, Monteverdi uses the dissonances to buttress the meaning of the word. In Figure 2.1, '*ahi lasso*', an exasperated ejaculation, is supported by the unprepared dissonances (ninth and seventh) that A and F in the vocal line of the soprano induce, in relation to the bass (G). In Figure 2.2, '*ma dell'aspido sordo*', meaning 'but deafer than a snake', is ornamented in stages using accenting, 'full of substitutions' of longer notes using notes of smaller value (Palisca, 1985, p. 132). Comparatively, this style of substituting notes of smaller value in place of longer ones is typically adopted in Karnatik music as sequences of ornamentation. Known as *sangatis*, these are iterations of the melodic line that are progressively complex. They follow the basic melodic contour of a line of text

Figure 2.1 Unprepared dissonances in '*Ahi Lasso*' m. 13 of *Cruda Amarilli* (1605).

Figure 2.2 Ornamental figures including *accenti* (accents), and *suppositi* (substitution) induced dissonances in *Cruda Amarilli*, mm. 35–38.

while allowing for variations at the note and phrasal levels. In doing so, they fuel virtuosic play within the seemingly rigid framework of the composition.

Known for their florid passages, the madrigals in question were not published until the *Fifth Book* (1605). However, the criticism, avoiding any text or mention of the composer by name, appeared in 1600. Monteverdi answered to Artusi in his letter in the preface to the *Fifth Book* (1605). He claimed that his new style, the *Seconda Prattica,* was dictated by the passions of the text. The words of Monteverdi's brother, Giulio Cesare, defending his brother's Second Practice, are an oft-quoted Platonian doctrine from the *Dichiaratione* of the *Scherzi Musicali* (1607): 'It has been [my brother's] intention to make the words the mistress of the harmony and not the servant' (trans. Strunk, 1950, p. 406). However, Monteverdi's one and only response (at the time) to his critics was through the letter in his *Fifth Book* (1605) which bore significance with regards to what the *Seconda Prattica* meant for his compositional intent. He declares that the second way of considering harmony is one that 'defends the modern manner of composition with the assent of the reason and senses' (trans. Palisca, 1985, p. 152), suggesting a blend of an analytical and affective approach to composition; one that looks to impact both the performer and listener. A coexistence of reason and senses is essentially the rightful interpretive balance of a work reimagined in the present that I referred to Section 1. This commitment to blending reason and convention with predisposition of creative sense and natural sensibility renders Monteverdi's compositional style interesting to unpack.

Overall, Monteverdi's *Seconda Prattica* was marked by daring dissonances, departures from modality, ornaments that were unsettling to consonant frameworks, and unconventional intervallic leaps – all to convey text with impact. In *Orfeo,* he applies these unique features of disobedience in conjunction with monody for drama. Non-conformance led to a new genre; however, it was never welcomed unopposed, as Monteverdi's run-ins with the Bolognese theorist Artusi evidence.

I now turn to consider the constructs that might have informed the vocal delivery of such compositions. A cursory glance at the theatrical cultures in Italy at the time is warranted to understand the role of expressive early modern singer-actors in relation to the music that was being made available to them for performance, such as Monteverdi's early operas.

Writing for Vocal Performers: Prevalent Vocal Performance Cultures in Italy

The prevalent performance cultures and their intersections with the singing-cum-acting abilities of the contemporary singers contributed significantly to the delivery of, and inspired the creation of, Monteverdi's musical dramas. The sixteenth century was indeed the age of the virtuosic singer in Italy (Wistreich, 1994, 2013).

Duke Vincenzo Gonzaga, Monteverdi's employer, was inspired by the '*concerto di donne*', the four singing ladies of Ferrara; he assembled his own team of the singing ladies of Mantua (Carter, 1999, pp. 88–89). Ferrarese singing was closely related to the madrigalist polyphonic style; the trend of ornamenting vocal lines was infectious and spilt over to monody writing of the times, rendering monody emblematic of virtuosic singing (Fenlon, 1986, p. 5; Newcomb, 1978).

Monteverdi's *lettere*, letters, reveal his bias towards the ornaments, *gorgie*, and *trillo*, as Wistreich's (1994, 2007, 2013) specialised articles on Monteverdi's singer evaluation and vocal style preferences reveal. The *gorgie* may be understood as the division of a note into diminutions using articulation of the throat in conjunction with the breath power from the chest. *Gorgie* are the life force behind the ornate *passaggi* that adorn Monteverdi's third-act strophic declamation model *Possente Spirto* from *L'Orfeo* (1607), or the *Audi Caelum* (from *Vespers*, 1610), for instance (Kurtzman, 2000). Carter (2012, p. 7) suggests that Monteverdi's approach to ornateness in the vocal writing in *Le Nozze di Telide*, 'a maritime fable', could be referred to as '*cantar di garbo* (florid style of singing)'. Carter (1984) points to the prevailing treatises of Bovicelli and Conforto that provided singers with 'possibilities in extemporised ornamentation', in referencing the importance of singers to the development of compositional styles at the time.

Carter (1999; 2002), and Fenlon (1985) observe that Monteverdi's inspiration for ornamentation could undoubtedly have been from the singers with whom he closely worked in *L'Orfeo*, specifically Francesco Rasi, who took on the title role. Rasi's composed collection of monodies that point to his familiarity with the embellished style of the time was aptly named *vaghezze di musica* (1608), referencing accented ornamentations of the time, *vaghezze*. Overall, ornamentation was a crucial factor in Monteverdi's writings for continuo-accompanied monody, and this he harnessed to expressive rhetoric, in the Orphic prayer, *Possente spirto*.

The dynamic theatrical culture of the sixteenth-century also provided Monteverdi and his contemporaries with models for rhetorical vocal delivery, acting, scenography, sets, costumes, and dancing (Carter, 2002, pp. 91–108). Monteverdi's attention to the germane extra-musical aspects, without which a representation of music as drama would be incomplete, was well acknowledged in his letters (Monteverdi & Stevens, 1980). The papal states of Florence, Ferrara, and Mantua, in healthy artistic competition with one another, were environments that held long traditions of pastoral plays, *intermedi*, and *commedia dell'arte* (Carter, 1993a; Pirrotta & Povoledo, 1982; Wilbourne, 2016). The first opera singers were professional actors, notes Calcagno (2002, p. 386), specifically citing the example of Virginia Ramponi Andreini, the first Arianna (Wilbourne, 2008).

Monteverdi would benefit greatly from the involvement of *commedia dell'arte* singers in his operas. Pastoral plays such as Guarini's *Il Pastor Fido* (1598) and the earliest secular play in Italian, Angelo Poliziano's *Fabula di Orfeo* (1480), contributed to theatrical ideas and themes for the future. *Intermedi*, which were performed vignettes between acts of spoken plays involving actors singing and dancing in elaborate costumes (for example, Girolamo Bargagli's *La Pellegrina*), were not only entertaining spectacles but also the training ground for performative singing (Ringer, 2006, pp. 7–8).

Monteverdi's first musical drama, *L'Orfeo*, was based on the Greek myth of the famed singer Orfeo who loses his wife Euridice, and tries, through music, to reclaim her from the underworld (Ringer, 2006, pp. 43–89). The Orphic theme was not new to the Italian performance scene; it harked back to Angelo Poliziano's dramatic representation *La favola di Orfeo* (the fable of Orfeo) of 1480. However, in 1607 it re-emerged from Monteverdi's diversely erected backdrop, aspects of which I have discussed earlier pertaining to declamation, the *Seconda Prattica*, virtuosic singing, acting, and dramatic performance cultures. Monteverdi's *L'Orfeo* was premiered on 24 February 1607, before the *Accademia degli invaghiti*, a group of aristocrat-scholars of the court (all men), who were experts in oration and versification (Schwindt, 2014).

Performance-Inflected Compositional Style

Based on Monteverdi's perceptible investment in the acting potential of his singers, and his care for word-clarity, I posit that his compositional language for dramatic voice derived from performance, and for performance. His compositional aesthetic melded the performer and the performative potential of poetry into the realm of performance. Therefore, I regard his compositional style, particularly for his operas, as *performance-inflected*, that is, influenced by and influencing vocal performance, rendering the style an exceptional approach for a singer-composer to reach for in order to reimagine the past and reinvigorate the present.

It is noteworthy that scholars refer to Monteverdi's dramatic writings in performative terms. Ossi (2003, p. 189), for instance, perceives his operatic language as derived from observing 'human nature'. Rosand (1991, p. 118) expresses his solo-song variants in relation to 'audience experience'; Nino Pirrotta, in terms of 'eloquent speech', referencing the rhetorical engagement with an audience

(Pirrotta & Povoledo 1982, p. 357); Fabbri (1994, p. 64) in terms of demands placed on the singers; and Fenlon (1985, p. 265) in terms of 'assimilation' and 'adaptation' of the singing style. All of them situate their discussion of his compositional style directly in performance, yet do not acknowledge this explicitly. One exception would be Calcagno (2002, 2012), whose ideas derive from the performative roots and implications in Monteverdi's music.

In the light of his monodies, Monteverdi's strategies are performance-stimulating affordances. They stem from a heightened awareness of what is being uttered in performance, who is uttering it, and why such an utterance might assume importance. I turn to Monteverdi's own ideas, as words; they indicate that the immediate practices and cultures around him were key to his style:

> I keep well away, in my writings, from that method upheld by the Greeks with their words and signs, employing instead the voices and characters we use in our practice, because my intention is to show by means of our practice what I have been able to extract from the mind of those philosophers for the benefit of good art. (Monteverdi, *lettera* dated 4 October 1634, in Monteverdi & Stevens, 1980, pp. 414–415)

Monteverdi's notated music houses 'supra-audible contents in musical artefacts from the past' (Abbate, 2004, p. 514) and in turn invites evaluation in conjunction with contemporary performance styles and affinities; a sense of artistic research travelling from the ancient time to Monteverdi's time, and into the present. The present, at each juncture, informs the creations by actively reshaping notions of the past.

Wistreich, in summing up several decades of Monteverdi studies, makes a pertinent observation that may situate the relevance of my current approach to Monteverdi in a 'wider cultural-historic' context: 'Until there is hermeneutics that is able to access the essential (but as yet barely tapped) embodied performative dimension in Monteverdi's music, historiography remains constrained by the limits of only reading (and listening to) the surviving texts of his compositions' (Wistreich, 2011, p. xxi). My current approach of interrogative artistic research aligns with this call to attention on Monteverdi's music, offering a current performer's perspective on a performance-inflected style of the past.

Overarching Musicality

Tutti gli interlocutori parlanno musicalmente

[all the actors shall speak musically]. (Solerti, 1904, p. 69 citing Carlo Magno)

If this statement from the letter of an attendee of the premiere of *L'Orfeo*, is anything to go by, it clearly underscores a musical approach to speech in *L'Orfeo*.

Terminology-wise, there were many ways in which composers and musicians of the time expressed music for drama. Representing song in performance, *stile rappresentativo*, was the term used by Caccini in his preface to his *Euridice* (1600); Monteverdi in his dedication to Vincenzo Gonzaga in the 1609 edition of *L'Orfeo* uses the phrase '*musicalmente rappresentata*', meaning performed/ represented in music (Carter, 2002, p. 120); Pietro Bardi interchangeably uses *stilo rappresentativo* and *musica rappresentativa* (Strunk, 1950, pp. 364–365). However, a clear bias towards musicality is evidenced in Monteverdi's slant in terminology – the word '*musica*' is made explicit in describing *L'Orfeo* (1607) as '*favola in musica*', a fable in music, even in the title. This aspect resonates with my key research question around reframing early opera: How can vocal ornamentation across cultures inform poetic delivery, musical intent, and drama? It is fortuitous that the theme of music is central to *L'Orfeo*; *La Musica* (music as a feminine form) introduces the tale, and Orfeo, the virtuosic singer, is the protagonist.

I hasten to acknowledge that Monteverdi's language for musical drama evolved over a period of thirty-six years, across two distinct cities: Mantua and Venice. The first two musical fables, *L'Orfeo* (1607) and *Arianna* (1608), were mythological, written for the court and nobility, in Mantua. The later three were written around three decades later for commercial Venetian opera: *Il ritorno d'Ulisse in Patria* (1640), *Le nozze d'Enea in Lavinia* (1641) (now lost), and *L'incoronazione di Poppea* (1643) (Rosand, 1991, 2007; Taruskin, 2010). With the establishment of the Teatro San Cassiano in the year 1637, opera came to Venice as a commercial activity, propelling the then–seventy-year-old Monteverdi once again into the limelight.

Even prior to the establishment of commercial opera, Monteverdi created opportunities for himself to dramatise poetry. As part of the *Eighth Book* (1638), *Madrigali guerrieri, et amorosi* (Madrigals of Love and War), he transformed narrative poetry into a dramatic *scena* in a few small works (*opuscoli*). These were in *genere rappresentativo* and included *Il Combattimento di Tancredi e Clorinda* and *Lamento della ninfa* (Taruskin, 2010, pp. 7–10). Taruskin (2010, p. 1) makes an astute observation of the operas across these two periods: 'they belonged to different genres', he declares. 'It was the second that actually bore the designation opera.' Due to the scope and objective of the current work, I have restricted myself to a discussion of only the first, *favola in musica*, in the context of voice, virtuosic ornamentation, intercultural interpretation, and the female performing body.

Overall, the seventeenth century was a time when newness was sought in performance practice; today researchers and performers are seeking fresh approaches to performance of early music. There is now a growing penchant for scholarship around reconsideration of the history of Western music from the perspective of cultural plurality and global mobility. Simultaneously there is an appetite for further musicological research across styles, not least in the light of the histories of cultural mobility during the early modern period.

I have thus far offered an overview of historical context and the unique musico-poetic style of operatic composition that Monteverdi championed. Section 3 will weave threads between granular specificities in musical style between Karnatik music and Monteverdian writing for opera. It will propose a framework that is grounded in comparative musicological analysis, affording a lattice structure for hybrid reimaginations to unfold.

3 Developing a Conceptual Framework for Hybridity

This Section adopts the approach of a comparative analysis. Drawing on the stances described earlier, I identify and compare unique features from Monteverdi's musico-rhetorical constructs with key elements of Karnatik music, in the context of declamation of poetry. I then propose a conceptual framework that consolidates the key themes that emerge from the comparison. This decahedral conceptual framework derives from theoretical and practical constructs. It envisions hybridity of the Karnatik singing style and Monteverdian declamation across ten stylistic levels. From melody, to ornamentation, to vocal delivery, the hybridity underscores the importance of emotion and ornamentation in vocal musical expression, across cultures.

My Musical Language: Karnatik Raga

In interpreting Monteverdi, I am trying to reach across four centuries and a cultural divide. To do this, I need to understand his musical language through mine.

(Author, journal entry, May 2016)

I understand Monteverdi's musical language for drama as a set of concepts, rather than literal devices. This is because his musical system is markedly different from mine. However, relating to it from a Karnatik perspective has also provided me with a lens to evaluate Karnatik raga from his musical paradigm. The envisaged two-way collaboration between the two musical declamatory styles, of the Karnatik and of Monteverdi, is well served by this model of cross-pollination.

I draw on the approach of composer Schachter (2015a, 2015b) to the comparative analysis of Karnatik and Western melodic material in informing my treatment of Karnatik raga in this analysis. I choose his approach for several reasons. It is a recent, well researched, and comprehensive comparative analysis of the Karnatik and Western musical systems and has been undertaken from a practical perspective. I draw on definitions for the Karnatik terminology used here from Widdess (1995, pp. 339–409), and Viswanathan and Allen (2004). Widdess (1995) discusses raga concepts from the ancient times and presents a thoroughly defined glossary of terms. Viswanathan and Allen (2004) use a simple pedagogical style designed for global audiences of Karnatik music. I cross-reference these perspectives with the knowledge acquired from my gurus and my performance experience. This self-knowledge component is known as *svanubhava* (self-experience) in Karnatik music and is acquired from years of *sadhana* (practice) (Krishna, 2013, pp. 193–199). As a practitioner-researcher I am able to bring this crucial component of knowledge into the research.

Turning to a description of Karnatik melodic material, a raga 'is a combination of musical heritage, technical elements, emotional charge, cognitive understanding, and aural identity' (Krishna, 2013, p. 56). It forms the staple of my musical language, and it is through this medium that I communicate with myself and with Monteverdi. Further exploration of Karnatik raga is warranted, in broad brushstrokes, at this juncture.

A raga in Karnatik music constitutes a set of pitches (*swarasthanas*) and their attendant microtonal ornaments (*gamaka*). The *swarasthana-gamaka* collective is a Karnatik note, the *swara*. The *swaras* occur in a specific order within an octave in any given raga. This repeatable order extends below and above the octave. Ragas usually contain seven, six, or five *swaras* to an octave. The ascent and descent of ragas may constitute the same set of *swaras* in the same order or vary in number and order of occurrence of *swaras*.

The pitches constitute not only an exacting pitch position (*swarasthana*, literally means 'place of *swara*'), but also the attendant ornamentation, *gamaka* (Krishna, 2013, pp. 45–48), as mentioned earlier. The *gamakas* embrace microtones before and after the theoretical *swara* positions, rendering a musical 'smearing' apparent in Karnatik music (Pearson, 2016b). Schachter (2015b, para. 4) refers to *gamaka* as the 'immediate aural experience of the listener', asserting its pre-eminence in the system. *Gamaka* is the signature sound of the Karnatik voice and conveys *bhava*; its application extends beyond its obvious functions of decoration and establishment of raga grammar (Pearson, 2016a, p. 48; Viswanathan, 1977, p. 31).

The defining features of the raga are its signature melodic motifs, the *prayogas*. Nettl (2009, pp. 42–43) draws on performer-scholar S. Ramanathan's approach to raga; he uses a few variants in terminology to describe *prayogas*: 'melodic themes', 'melodic fragments', 'segments', and 'character'. *Prayogas* is the preferred term when these motifs are short; the term *sancharas* is used when the motifs are concatenated to slightly longer contours. Together, *gamakas, swaras, prayogas*, and *sancharas* build a raga.

Schachter (2015b, para. 4–5) proposes a hierarchical model to explain the levels of organisation in Karnatik music. He progresses from *gamaka* to *swara*, to *prayoga* (short signature phrases), and through to the broadest construct, a holistic representation of raga. A comparable approach to *gamaka, swara*, and *prayoga* is seen in Pearson's (2016a, p. 83) argument for co-articulatory gestures in Karnatik music; 'individual svaras in Karnatak music are subsumed under larger gestural units', she writes. Drawing from Godøy (2011, p. 67), she contrasts the 'atomistic' (theoretical *swara* positions) to the larger holistic structures *(swara-gamaka* combinations, *prayogas*, and *sancharas*), the 'gestural sonic-events' (Pearson 2016a, p. 83). Therefore, the trajectory from *swara-gamaka* combination to *prayoga* and finally to broad raga structure progresses from the micro to the macro level in the hierarchical organisation of the melodic material in Karnatik music. In my Karnatik transactions with Monteverdi's music I propose to harness the *swara*-based perspective to the continuity that a gestural motif perspective offers.

Theoretically, an octave in Karnatik music is separated into twenty-two microtones (twenty-two *srutis*), yielding unequal intervals of whole and half steps. Schachter (2015b, para. 16, footnote 6) notes, 'in practice, however, vocalists and instrumentalists tune *svaras* more closely to just intervals over the fundamental' tonic, resulting in a closer association with the Western semitonal separation in tuning. Empirical research, however, has shown that Karnatik pitch as performed in practice (with *gamakas*) does not simply conform to *Just Intonation*, equal temperament, or the twenty-two *sruti* theory (Komaragiri, 2011, p. 15; M. Subramanian, 2002). Drawing on my experiences with hybridity in Karnatik practice, wherein artists often perform with chordal accompaniment provided by Western instruments in fusion settings, I express intervals between *swarasthana* positions in terms of semitonal approximations (and Western scale positions, such as minor third, major third, etc.) in my visual representations and discussions. This approach of approximation to communicate broader musical intent and content is also supported by Pesch (1999, p. 95) as one effective way to communicate *swara* positions to Western musicians.

In Table 3.1, I present the twelve *swara* positions in an octave, their *solfège* (each approximately separated by a semitone), and their sixteen names (four

Table 3.1 Pitch positions in Karnatik music within an octave: 12 positions, 16 names, 7 scale degrees and their relationship to the Western musical system

Pitch position	Scale degree	Swara solfége	Swara name	Western term
1	1	Sa	Sadja	Tonic
2	2	Ri (1)	Suddha Rishabha	Second (minor)
3	2	Ri (2)/Ga (1)	Chatusruti Rishabha /Suddha Gandhara (En. rare)	Second (major)
4	3	Ri (3)/Ga (2)	Shatsruti Rishabha (En. rare)/ Sadharana Gandhara	Third (minor)
5	3	Ga (3)	Antara Gandhara	Third (major)
6	4	Ma (1)	Suddha Madhyama	Fourth (perfect)
7	4	Ma (2)	Prati Madhyama	Fourth (augmented)
8	5	Pa	Pancama	Perfect fifth
9	6	Dha (1)	Suddha Dhaivata	Sixth (minor)
10	6	Dha (2)/Ni (1)	Chatusruti Dhaivata/ Suddha Nishada (En. rare)	Sixth (major)
11	7	Dha (3)/Ni (2)	Shatsruti Dhaivata (En. rare)/ Kaisikhi Nishada	Seventh (minor)
12	7	Ni (3)	Kakali Nishada	Seventh (major)

enharmonic). There are three variants to the second, third, sixth, and seventh scale degrees (with two overlapping positions on each scale degree), and two variants to the fourth; the tonic and the fifth are fixed. The variants are indicated as numbers in brackets. The enharmonics are seen only in a small selection of ragas that are known as *vivadi* (dissonant) ragas. I have indicated enharmonic notes in Table 3.1 as 'en'.

The systematisation of raga into seventy-two possible *melakarta*s, each with a seven-*swara* arrangement, was effected by theorist Venkatamakhi around 1660 through his treatise *Chaturdanti Prakashika*. The tonic and the perfect fifth (dominant) in his scheme are fixed and are approximately seven semitones apart. The upper tetrachord between the dominant and the octave constitutes approximately five semitones between its four notes. While *melakartas* are 'parent' scales that possess all seven notes in both ascent and descent (as mirror images of one another), the derived 'child' ragas, the *janyas*, are those that miss one or two notes in ascent or descent, or both. They still progress stepwise, eschewing the scale degrees that their pitch positions do not correspond to. Some of the *janyas* could move 'crookedly' as *vakra*, 'starting to move in one direction then temporarily reversing direction before continuing in the original direction' (Viswanathan & Allen, 2004, p. 43).

I do not delve into the *melakarta* system in this book; it is a very broad, well-researched subject (Krishna, 2013, pp. 439–449; Pesch, 1999, pp. 93–105; Sambamoorthy, 1964). I refer to this system as a background for the ragas that surface in the musical processes. In extrapolating parallels between Western and Karnatik music, I hasten to acknowledge the possible risk of a reductivist approach. I concur with Schachter's (2015b) view, and steer away from analogies that are based on oversimplification, as far as possible: '[As] I frequently point out when Western and Karnatak musical elements or concepts overlap; I must stress that all such cross-comparisons are approximate analogies, whose sole purpose is to give readers better versed in one tradition a more immediate reference for understanding the other' (Schachter, 2015b, para. 9).

The semitonal approximations are a stretch from raga theory since Karnatik music does not follow equal temperament. However, the continuity between *swaras* that is manifest due to the microtonal *gamakas* has rendered even established theoretical concepts, such as twenty-two *srutis* (microtones) to an octave, far removed from actual raga-music practice, as Komaragiri (2013) establishes.

I reiterate that, in practice, a communication of a raga's scalar structure through semitonal separations between *swarasthanas* (pitch positions) might be a workable model to communicate raga across cultures, as Pesch (1999, p. 95) also infers. I also believe that supplementary media with practical examples might be helpful in mitigating the risk of obfuscation in such approximations. In my approach to raga, I resonate with Wade's observation of the Karnatik tradition; I privilege my practical knowledge: 'South Indian tradition encompasses more possibilities that are current. There is so much evidence that flexibility in practice is the rule rather than the exception, that performance practice must be given the final word in any discussion' (Wade, 1979, p. 87).

Having laid out certain tenets from which my approach to the Karnatik element of melody shall emerge, I now begin to describe the decahedral framework of hybridity that I have developed in the light of the theoretical and practical aspects of both practices. In the context of artistic research, this conceptual framework serves two important purposes: It 'deterritorialises' the two musical practices by resituating them into the third space of 'reciprocity', as Coessens et al. (2009, pp. 63–64) propose for ARiM (Artistic Research in Music). It also serves to transport my Self and identity into the zone of 'play'.

The Decahedral Framework of Hybridity

I identify ten areas as the key intersections of features in Monteverdi's compositional style and the Karnatik musico-poetic form, the *Viruttam*.

1. Rhetorical style and construct of form
2. Poetic construct
3. Syllabic forward motion and *laya*
4. Melodic material: Modality, tonality, and raga
5. Consonance and dissonance as dramatic devices
6. Continuo and the harmonic sphere of *prayoga*
7. Ornamentation
8. Instrumentation
9. *Oratione*, affect, and *rasa*
10. *Sprezzatura* and *Sowkhya*

These are represented in Figure 3.1 as a decahedral conceptual framework with the performing body at the epicentre. I arrived at this framework by identifying the prominent nodes of resonances across the key aspects of musical form, structure, text, melody, notions of time, vocal delivery, instrumentation, and, importantly, feeling – as affect and *bhava* – across Karnatik music and Monteverdi's declamatory compositional practice for musical drama. The following themed discussion expands on each of the conceptual parameters and their relationship to the musical practices under scrutiny here. The framework thus delineated provides a consolidated comparison of both musical practices and acts as a precursor, substrate, and resource for the ensuing interrogation through practical hybridisation.

Rhetorical Style and Construct of Musical Form

Joachim Steinheuer (2007) pioneered the mapping of Monteverdi's musical organisation, in declamation, across stylistic levels of rhetoric. In doing so, he established the linkage between composed form and persuasive delivery, with dramatic impact at the centre. Schwindt (2014) contributed further to this scholarship in arguing that Monteverdi was well versed with rhetoric. He drew on the content and tone of Monteverdi's letters.

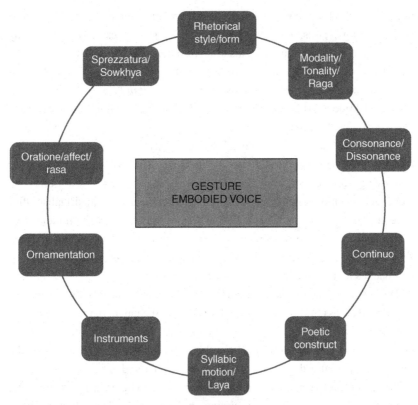

Figure 3.1 Decahedral conceptual framework for hybridisation

These isolated bodies of scholarship contribute to a greater discourse related to the Baroque itself. Composition was linked to performance in the Baroque, not least in the monody tradition for drama. The lines between performers and composers, and improvisation and composition, were blurred at the time, as much scholarship affirms (Cyr, 2017; Haynes, 2007). Recent trends in the study of creativity in music emphasise the decentralisation of creativity from the locus of composition to its broadest possible manifestations – as improvised moments in performance, as distributed manifestations of musical ideas through embodied gesture, and as varieties in sound (Cook, 2018; Crispin, 2013, 2015; Leech-Wilkinson & Prior, 2014). As a collective response to these interrelated bodies of scholarship that relate to delivery and creative impact in the proposed hybridity, I introduce the idea of mapping rhetorical styles to musical organisation.

A glance at the rhetorical styles that come to bear on the selection of a sung-speech approach or a spoken-song approach to declamation is war-ranted here. Steinheuer (2007, p. 139) explains that the 'high style level' of rhetoric is an elevated style that is instructive and pertains to higher things, such as kings, gods, celestial beings, and moral issues. It is marked by a delivery without ornaments. This style of delivery emphasises text entirely, and therefore I align it, for the purposes of classification, with the *recitar cantando* model. The intersections of *recitar cantando* and the high level rhetorical style mark specific pieces in *L'Orfeo*, including the *La Musica* (*Prologo*) and *Rosa del ciel.*

Steinheuer (2007, p. 139) refers to the 'middle style level' rhetoric as one that delights the listeners, but fails to move them. The delighting happens by employing ornateness and replete passagework. This style refers to a declamatory model with continuous melisma, indicative of madrigalist influence, as exemplified in *Possente Spirto.* I conceptually map the middle style level of rhetoric to the spoken-song style, *cantar recitando,* alluded to earlier. This could be regarded as a melodic expansion on *recitar cantando,* in that it approaches text from a musically intensive angle.

The rhetorical styles and their correspondences with speech-song forms can be mapped across to Karnatik music. By adopting the length of raga phrases and ornaments as variable parameters, as well as by using the voice and *gamaka* to enunciate text and passion concurrently, a certain rhetorical intent may be introduced within a declamation. This intent is derived from a performance-inflected perspective and could once again translate to delivery in performance. Haynes and Burgess's (2016) discussion on declamation clearly highlights the link to the performative in declamation:

> Heightened speech served as the primary model for musicians in the Rhetorical age. Singers were an important point of contact and were normally thought of as actors. They had to make sure their listeners heard and understood the text – not just the individual words, but what those words implied and their underlying passion. The necessity to make every word understandable in what amounts to 'musical declamation' affects many aspects of a singer's delivery, not least their diction. (Haynes & Burgess, 2016, p. 144)

Figure 3.2 depicts the zone of hybridity conceived in this research in relation to rhetorical styles and compositional strategies.

For the hybridity to reside in the zone that ranges melodically from just beyond *recitar cantando* to just beyond *cantar recitando,* the melodic material continuum would need to range from the very simple (smaller *prayogas* and less *gamaka*) to the slightly complex (longer *prayogas* and *sancharas,* and more *gamaka*). The challenge would be to achieve the hybridity without a significant drop in textual prominence across these two stylistic levels. The area in Figure 3.2 is a 'sweet spot' where text and melody could interact with each other such that neither eclipses the rhetorical function of the other. Further,

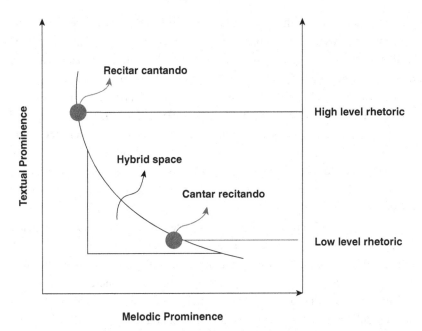

Figure 3.2 Rhetorical styles and musical form mapped to text-melody relationship

Figure 3.2 indicates that the melodic complexity in this zone lies much beyond the simpler sung-speech (*recitar cantando*) style of Monteverdian high-level rhetoric, while being comparable to the spoken-song (*cantar recitando*) madrigalist style of the times. Thereby, the continuum, envisaged here as the seat of hybridity, can arguably accommodate both the dramatisation of *Viruttam* and the Karnaticisation (making sound Karnatik) of declamation.

Melodic Material: Modality, Tonality, and Ragas

Modality and its intersections with tonality, in Monteverdi's practice, may be contextualised in Karnatik music by regarding raga as being comparable with a mode. Changing tonal spheres may be considered as either a 'garland of ragas' or as shifts in tonicity within a raga. This is because, when there is a tonality shift, such a shift often suggests a set of ragas based on the ways in which the tonic is imagined, and the octave is envisaged by the listener or performer who might be more familiar with Karnatik ragas than with Western tonalities. When every such shift suggests a raga, a continually shifting spectrum of tonal clusters (as is common in the case of Monteverdi's music) induces a sense of a string of various ragas.

Over the years, scholars have identified ragas with Renaissance modes. Notable of them is Harold S. Powers (1958a, 1958b); '[ragas and modes] are alike in that they are both based on melodic formulas and associated with scale systems', he observes (1958b, p. 459). He also, however, identifies a basic difference between ragas and modes; he notes, 'Western modes show virtually a one-to-one correspondence with the scales of the system, whereas in the South Indian system there are not only theoretical scales with no ragas in them but also theoretical scales with more than one raga' (1958b, p. 460). Viswanathan and Allen (2004, p. 53) present a comparative tablature between the eight Renaissance modes and ragas, a model that has been popular in intercultural raga mappings for several decades. The modality in Monteverdi's approach is arguably a fascinating starting point for musical encounters with raga-based music.

Steinheuer (2007, pp. 126–140) demonstrates Monteverdi's use of modality alongside departures into tonality as a 'complex system of reference in which musical codes are assigned to semantic layers' (p. 131). In his analyses of *Possente Spirto*, for instance, he assigns the tonal spheres of A major, A minor, and E major to the underworld and death, drawing on the dissonances and modulations within the *messeggiera's* announcement. G Dorian, with a strong tonal centre at G minor is assigned to *Orfeo* across his declaration of love in *Rosa del ciel*, to his Act III plea, *Possente*, his lament in Act V, well into his duet final with his father, Apollo, that marks his departure to heaven. However, despite their theoretical modal unity, the departures from the mode into tonal clusters of signification render each of the above listed Orphic declamatory moments uniquely tied to various dramatic instances.

Rosa del ciel aligns with the G Dorian and signifies Orfeo's state of harmony with all things in the world at that point in the story – his love for Euridice, the sunny world and his singing Self. In *Possente Spirto*, the tonal spheres move around. The word '*Spirto*', for instance, meanders through an ornament to the fourth before plunging into the dissonant second. The reference to Caronte as 'god' in the word '*nume*' expresses intensity through the appearance of a destabilising seventh. Overarchingly, dissonance and modulation in seventeenth-century music relate to the sense of moving tonal centres. Eric Chafe (1992, p. 4) notes that Monteverdi invoked and reinforced his changing-tonal-centre model by using 'hierarchical harmonic devices' such as an 'array of cadences'.

Such a reinforcement may be analogised to the *prayogas* in a raga tending towards the central *amsa swara*, the note of departure and often resolution of a phrasal motif. As the raga changes, so do its *amsa* and *nyasa* (ending *swara* of a cadence) scale degrees, indicative of the rationale behind tonicity. Even within a raga, different *prayogas* attract different cadential resolutions when elaborated within the grammatical confines of their harmonic regions.

Karnatik ragas, therefore, despite being modal in nature, provide the possibility of being dissected into harmonic regions that may thrive independently of one another, albeit for only a short time. They must return to the point of departure, the raga's *amsa swara*; however, each harmonic region can enjoy its short-lived autonomy through *prayogas* and *sancharas* woven within them. The harmonic regions marked by the *prayogas* could yield chords that underline the vocal line, an attribute that could greatly benefit the hybrid approach being discussed here. Together, the *prayogas* of the vocal line and the underscoring chords could create tonal centres which may hold rhetorical and emotional significance.

I take an example of raga *Shanmukhapriya* (see Kaufmann, 1976, p. 592) to illustrate the various harmonic zones possible in a raga (Audio 3.1) This raga constitutes a major second, a minor third, sixth and seventh, an augmented fourth, and a perfect fifth. As the clip indicates, the switch between the minor and major tonalities of the third scale degree renders the interaction between the augmented fourth and the perfect fifth, typical of the raga, as a dynamic and flowing interweaving of the dark and the light shades in the raga. In terms of figured bass, the 6/3 and the usual 5/3 from the tonic as the root position enact the duality between the unrest in the minor sixth scale degree and the temporary comfort provided by the minor tonic triad. The 4/3 relationship from the second scale degree, when modulated into the tonic triad, showcases the destabilising second–augmented fourth–minor sixth relation in juxtaposition against the stabilising tonic-minor third–fifth relation. Therefore, multiple tonal spheres are perceptible within regions of a raga. Figure 3.3 is a scalar version of pitch positions in *Shanmukhapriya* showing possible harmonic spheres.

It must be noted that the chordal substrates notated in Figure 3.3 are not representative of Karnatik music practice or theory, but are rather of my own devising as part of the hybrid approach to the research. Monteverdi's approach to harmony – both modal and tonal – can be explored from the perspective of a single raga, as explained using the previous *Shanmukhapriya* example. However, there emerges another approach to introducing varying tonalities within a single raga. By adopting a raga that uses accidentals, momentary defections from a tonal sphere to another can be effected. Defined by Widdess (1995, p. 398) as 'notes that are temporarily sharpened or flattened', the accidentals are connected to the concept of foreign notes (*bhashanga swaras*)

Audio 3.1 Tonal spheres in raga Shanmukhapriya. Audio available in online formats.

Shanmukhapriya

Figure 3.3 Chordal substrate possibilities for raga *Shanmukhapriya*.

in Karnatik music. Certain ragas use foreign notes as part of their grammatical construct (e.g., raga *Kapi*). In the case of *Kapi*, as Pesch (2016) notes, the foreign note is not an accidental, but fulfils the function of one. This is because, while the foreign note is not part of the parent *melakarta* raga, it is a distinguishing addition to the derived *janya* raga.

The scope for varying tonalities within a single raga is limited; only the *swara*s that grammatically belong to the raga may feature in the vocal line or in the bass line, at any point. This leaves the composer with fewer options compared to another more fertile scenario, described in the following.

This other scenario involves exploration using multiple ragas and affords almost unlimited scope for varying tonalities. Additionally, the affective qualities of each of the interwoven ragas and the intervallic structures that are typical to each of them complement the overall soundscape. In this scenario, Monteverdi's departures from the mode into tonal spheres can be regarded in relation to a parallel concept, *ragamalika*, a garland of many ragas. Regardless of the ragas that are featured in a Karnatik concert, the tonic-drone (*tanpura*) maintains a constant tonicity throughout a Karnatik music concert, rendering the intervallic relationship between the constitutive *swaras* of a raga very important. When every verse of poetry in a *Viruttam* is assigned to a different raga, this design of musical organisation abets *ragamalika* (Vedavalli, 2011). However, even within a single verse, multiple ragas may be interwoven. This is considered complex; however, it is achievable, and is closest to Monteverdi's approach to dynamically evolving melodic material.

Monteverdi's modal departures could also be seen as parallel to the temporary 'shift of tonic' approach in Karnatik music. The shift of tonic that is common in

Audio 3.2 Shift of tonic: Grahabhedam in raga Abhogi. Audio available in online formats.

Graha Bhedam

Figure 3.4 Graha Bhedam: The fourth scale degree of the raga *Abhogi* when assuming tonicity, becomes raga *Valaji*.

Karnatik music is known by the term *graha-bhedam*. Referred to also as *sruti-bhedam*, it literally translates to 'a modal shift of tonic' (Pesch, 1999, p. 94). An example of such a shift is seen in ragas where the fourth scale degree is powerful and attracts temporary tonicity. In such a case, the plagal relationship between the fourth and its fifth higher immediately comes into operation, invoking a transposed raga. For instance, when the fourth scale degree of a certain penta-tonic raga, known as *Abhogi*, assumes tonicity, a raga known as *Valaji* emerges. In Audio 3.2, I journey briefly into *graha-bhedam* between *Abhogi* and *Valaji*, to illustrate this principle; Figure 3.4 is a scalar depiction of this media.

Figures 3.3 and 3.4 use Western staff notation to show pitch positions and their occurrences in chord-making and tonic-shift, respectively. They do not, however, do justice to the nature of *gamaka*-imbued *swara*s. The audio examples, therefore, are the holders of the raga's essential quality; not the notation segments.

While *graha-bhedam* presents one pathway through which a raga can change into another, there are other ways in which a similar sense of changing ragas can be affected. One raga can move into another by shifting the harmony of the bass line at the point in question. This approach would alter the tonal organisation at the harmonic substrate level and this alteration would translate to the vocal line; not vice versa, as the previous approaches illustrate.

In the discussion here, I expanded on Karnatik ragas and their correspond-ences with tonality and modality. This facet relating to melody is the first of ten to contribute to the decahedron of hybridity.

Consonance and Dissonance as Dramatic Devices

I extend the discussion on melodic material, modality, and tonality into a glance at the way in which the features of consonance and dissonance in Monteverdi's approach align with those of Karnatik ragas. The theory and practice of Indian music has a well-developed sense of consonance and dissonance. The *prayogas* play a major role in determining the *swara* combinations of resolution, conson-ance, and dissonance, including the typical cadential tendencies of the raga, as discussed earlier.

Amsa, the most important *swara* in a raga, is also regarded as the *graha swara*, the note where most *prayogas* begin. This *swara* could also be the *vadi*, a strong note in the raga. This note assumes strength from the consonant fourth or perfect fifth, known as the *samvadi*. The *anuvadi* functions as an assonant, neither consonant *(samvadi)* nor dissonant *(vivadi)*. Imagining these notes in a Western context, along with the *anuvadi*, the *vadi* and *samvadi* could form harmonic spheres, as chords (Morris & Ravikiran, 2006, pp. 267–268). I elaborate further on this method of creating chords using the linearity of raga, by practically demonstrating the use of figured bass using raga in the artistic processes.

The concept of dissonance in Karnatik music differs from the concept as seen in seventeenth-century Western music. The appearance of a note that does not accord with the harmony in relation to the chord constructed by the bass note was regarded as a dissonance in Monteverdi's time. It was resolved by directing the voice, usually by step to the next chord tone, or by moving the bass to form a different chord (Cyr, 2017, pp. 71–73).

The Karnatik concept of dissonance defined by the term *vivadi,* in contrast, is defined in relation to the interval between one *swara* and the next, and not evaluated with regards to the relationship between a *swara* and a chordal substrate. This is because the concept of harmonic substrate does not exist in Karnatik music; it is a linearly progressive music system.

As Widdess (1995, p. 409) notes, a *swara* is said to be a *vivadi* with respect to another if its position is approximately one semitone removed from the neigh-bouring *swara*. Although Widdess' explanation of *vivadi* is in relation to North Indian Classical music, it applies to Karnatik music as well, and in the Karnatik music the *vivadi* experience is practically realised through *gamaka* ornamenta-tion. The semitone-based definition of *vivadi* could also be extended to the separation of a *swara* from the fundamentals suggested by the drone (the tonic, fifth, and octave), engendering a comparable harshness. In the case of an underlying continuo constructed using a combination of *vadi*, *samvadi* and *anuvadi swaras*, a *vivadi* dissonance effect could be designed through a clash between the vocal line and the bass line, or by using a chromatic descent of the bass line against a vocal line, or vice versa.

Comparing with Monteverdi's approach to dissonance and resolution, it is possible to buttress moments of textual intensity by introducing a *swara* (and its attendant ornament) that is very close to the fifth or the tonic at pivotal times. The augmented fourth, known as the *prati madhyama*, is an ideal candidate. The ornaments, with their microtonal inflections, could also give rise to a feeling of dissonance as the figures of ornamentation from *Cruda Amarilli* earlier demonstrated (see Figure 2.2, again).

In Monteverdi's style, the dissonances may move towards a stable chord or vice versa; likewise, in Karnatik music, unstable notes such as the *prati madhyama* seek resolution by moving towards a stable *swara* such as the fifth, as the earlier example from raga *Shanmukhapriya* illustrates (see Audio 3.1).

Resolution in raga might happen across a series of *swara* degrees, often drawn out across *prayogas*. For instance, in Audio 3.1, the tension erected using the augmented fourth resolves after intensifying across the seventh and sixth scale degrees. Likewise, Monteverdi's dissonances often linger on in a bittersweet domain before meandering through a series of scale degrees, invoking uncomfortable intervals, and inching towards the much-awaited resolution.

A case in point is the opening line of *Arianna's* lament (1608), *Lasciatemi morire* (see Figure 3.5). The ominous minor sixth (B♭ in this case) creeps up on the A minor tonality, thereby invoking the dissonant ninth, which resolves temporarily as the bass note inches towards the G minor tonality. The B♭ assumes the role of a minor third in '*lasciatemi*', 'let me'. The anticipation of the listener reaches a climax when '*morire*', 'to die', is intoned in an unstable second scale degree. But that is not all. A leap from the second scale degree to the major sixth meanders through the C♮ and C♯ to the octave, declaring with vehemence Arianna's will to die. The leap quietens after only a moment's vacillation at the second, the tonal centre, D.

The ways in which Monteverdi resolves his dissonances, an example of which *Lasciatemi* depicted, show that his designs are not always conventional (de Goede, 2005). The pre-tonal explorations of chordal harmony engendered unusual intervals – augmented, diminished, and chromatic – in his style.

Monteverdi's musical intervals were unlike Renaissance intervals, and if I may advance the idea, closer to the intervals perceived in the *swara*

Figure 3.5 Situating features of *Seconda Prattica* into a dramatic domain: The opening bars of Monteverdi's (1614/1623) *Lasciateme morire* from *Arianna* (1608).

arrangement of certain ragas that contain augmented fourths and raised/natural sevenths. When a long note (*karvai*) is held over the bass line inducing intervals that are unstable, the effect could arguably be close to what a Western dissonance might induce.

The appearance of the unprepared seventh in *Cruda Amarilli* bothered Artusi, as seen in the earlier section (Figure 2.1). In parallel, in Karnatik theory, the seventh scale degree denoted by the *swara*-solfége 'Ni', is associated with discomfort and a yearning for resolution, as Mudaliyar (1893/1982, p. 13) observes: ' '*Ni*' is the yell of the Elephant with his extended proboscis when the Mahout attacks the back of his head with a scimitar'. Likewise, the second, fourth (particularly the augmented variant), and the sixth are also regarded as unstable in Karnatik theory. Mudaliyar (1893/1982) confirms that images of animals in pain or in various states of anxiety have been used by theorists to illustrate these unstable positions. Interestingly, ragas and *prayogas* with unstable notes abound in Karnatik music, and are considered as normative as ragas that do not.

The ubiquitous presence of the *adhara sruti*, the *tanpura* drone, is a key feature of Karnatik music. The tonic-fifth-octave combination, as stated earlier, is provided by the plucked instrument, the *tanpura*, and is described by H. S. Powers (1958b) as 'an extra, quasi-harmonic dimension to Indian modality' (p. 456). The pitch positions in a Karnatik raga interact not only with each other, but are also in an interval-based relationship with the *tanpura sruti*. Schachter (2015b, para. 23, footnote 11) states that 'it is not clear whether performers that keep the sa-pa-sa drone in these cases do so out of a desire to intentionally create tension against the raga or out of inertia'. My personal experience encourages me to take the former view. The potential for tension–resolution in raga is buttressed due to the drone and can be harnessed in the context of highlighting textual meaning in the hybrid.

In sum, this facet of the decahedral framework relates to the principles of consonance and dissonance in Monteverdi's approach and their alignment with comparable features in Karnatik raga, opening up yet another dimension for hybridity.

Continuo and the Harmonic Sphere of Prayoga

In 1602, Caccini's *Le Nuove Musiche* (Caccini, 1602/2009a) emerged with its many proposed compositional, didactic, and singing solutions. With it, the continuo accompaniment emerged as the harmonic and rhythmic frame for the solo song. In using continuo, termed by Price (1993) as a 'prized product of the intersection of the *recitar cantando* and the *seconda prattica*' (p. 10), the accompaniment to the vocal line was reduced to a single line and figures. A bass note with figures indicated the notes above the root that should feature in creating the chord. Its primary function was to provide harmonic support for the overlaid voice.

Madrigals anticipate the continuo in Monteverdi's monodies for drama. Monteverdi's first engagement with figured bass was in his *Fifth Book* (1605), and the trend of using a bass line to underscore the voice continued into his dramas. The vocal line enjoyed freeness while the harmonic and rhythmic fundamentals were safely consigned to the continuo; this arrangement was highly suited for the strophic declamation models in *L'Orfeo*.

Lawrence-King (2014) observes that it is the continuo that leads forward the voice in the declamations in *L'Orfeo*, and not vice versa. Pirrotta (1984, p. 228) declares it a foil to vocal expressivity; 'the advent of the basso continuo made possible an even more precise correspondence between particular phrases of text and music', he observes, rendering its function in this research highly pertinent to textual primacy. The continuo, therefore, functions not only as a harmonic substrate but also as a regulator of rhythm; it is in constant interaction with the word, highlighting and guiding it, when it matters.

The *Prologo* and *Possente Spirto* from *L'Orfeo* are examples in which the vocal line varies over a bass-line schema that is fairly constant. These are 'strophic variation forms', which Carter (2002, p. 29) identifies as settings 'with more or less the same bass line, and therefore harmonic scheme, but with the melody altered to suit the text'.

The variations in the vocal melodic lines between stanzas are more pronounced in *Possente Spirto* due to its highly embellished melodic figures. *Possente Spirto* is a strophic variation model of six stanzas, each of three lines; it is a classic *terza rima* structure that is handled with freeness over a repeated bass pattern (Steinheuer, 2007, p. 134–136). The *Prologo* incorporates simpler variations in the vocal line, and is a strophic variation model of five stanzas, each constructed as a strophic quatrain over a sixteen-note bass scheme per stanza (Carter, 2002, p. 29). A key feature of the continuo is that it renders the overlaid monody conducive for improvisation. It is this very feature that renders it interesting from a Karnatik perspective.

Chitravina Ravikiran drawing on his 'melharmony' project establishes that even subtle variations in raga phrases can vary the emotion conveyed significantly; 'in Indian music, a wide variety of moods can be projected by a small change in sequence within a raga' (Ravikiran & Morris, 2014, p. 157). Such variations could be overlaid on a harmonic substrate generated using raga notes. In the context of continuo-voice interaction, this overlay could demonstrate the effectiveness of raga-derived continuo in inducing a wide spectrum of emotions in combination with the vocal monody. A Karnatik approach of generating variations in the vocal line (*sangatis*) can inform both generative creativity and emotion in the hybridisation. In sum, this facet of the decahedral framework extrapolates the principles of continuo accompaniment in Monteverdi's approach into the realm of Karnatik music, creating yet another pathway for hybridity to emerge.

Poetic Construct

This dimension of hybridity relates the nature of poetry in the Monteverdian style to the poetic structure in the Tamil language, the primary language of musical declamation in Karnatik music. The bass-line in the Monteverdian approach to composition for poetry not only dictates harmonic progression; its relationship to the syllables of the vocal line is of crucial importance. The bass notes are often elongated or truncated as per the length of syllables and the accents. The poetry therefore dictates the number of bass notes, as Steinheuer (2007, pp. 134–137) observes.

Turning towards Karnatik music, historical connotations of the word *Viruttam* reveal the form's close association with poetic metre. *Viruttam* etymologically derives from the Sanskrit term *vrtta*, meaning metre. Peterson (1989, p. 65) notes that the terms *vrtta*, *itivrtta*, and *vrttanta* mean 'narration of events', revealing the form's connections with drama. Apte (1970) establishes that Sanskrit poetry follows syllabic metres or *aksharas,* and is based on the constancy of the *number* of syllables in a line. In contrast, he notes that moric metres pertain to constancy in the *duration* of syllables within a line. Usually, in Tamil poetry, the duration of the metric feet remains constant (Zvelebil, 1973, p. 275), mapping to Moric metre. By comparison, in Sanskrit *Vrtta* and in the Italian poetry that Monteverdi and his contemporaries dealt with (including those of Guarini, Chiabrera, Rinuccini, and Striggio) the number of syllables in a line remain constant (syllabic metre).

Striggio, in his verses for *L'Orfeo,* follows the established poetry conventions of the time established by Rinuccini and Chiabrera (Tomlinson, 1987, pp. 114–147). Each line of the quatrain of the *Prologo*, for instance, houses eleven syllables of varied mensuration, abetting the well-known *endecasibillo* structure (Carter, 2002, pp. 47–73).

This basic difference in poetic construct between Tamil poetry and Italian poetry would mean that the bass notes in the Tamil poetry would correspond to the duration of the feet, and not necessarily to the number of syllables. However, a relatively free structural construction of the bass line allows for adjustments pertaining to syllable-related and duration-related issues. This flexibility renders a conceptual mapping and hybridity of Karnatik declamation and Monteverdian declamation possible through a leveraging of the facet of poetic construct in the decahedral framework.

Syllabic Forward Motion and Laya

In terms of forward motion of the musico-poetic form, the role of the continuo as a regulatory device that aids in harmony and rhythm has been discussed. However, a more nuanced concept resides at the heart of the notion of time and rhythm across both practices of declamation. The concept of Karnatik time-keeping, *tala*, is much researched, particularly in the West. *Tala* is expressed primarily as cyclic metrical patterns, and time in *tala* is kept using the hands (Pesch, 1999, pp. 128–133). However, there is another concept of time in Karnatik music, *laya*, through which time is expressed in abstract terms (Bailey, 1992, p. 3–5; Krishna, 2013, pp. 61–63). Bailey (1992, p. 4) describes *laya* as 'rhythmic impetus, and a sense of forward motion'; the 'all embracing comprehensive rhythm of the universe'. Based on my experience, I concur with Krishna's (2013, p. 61) description of *laya*; he notes, 'speed [or slowness] is a sense, a feeling, and a conditioning . . . in Karnatak music speed is not equal to a mathematical value'.

The writings on tempo in the early Baroque note that a syllable-led style marked the declamation models in early opera (Cyr, 2017; Grant, 2014; Lawrence-King, 2015, 2017). In this style, as well as in the concept of *laya*, especially in the *Viruttam* or in the simpler declamatory variant, known as *Slokam*, time is dictated by the poetic metre and the inflections in delivery, not as repeating units of time-values.

The absence of a conductor in the early Baroque opera and the emergence of the continuo as an agency of forward motion are two features that align with the concept of rhythmic flexibility within declamation. Lawrence-King (2015, p. 126) connects Caccini's *sensa misura* (without measures) style – 'the singer floating in a cool way, over a regular bass' – to moments in *Possente Spirto*. The *sensa misura* idea offers the experimental possibility of composing and performing without barlines, thereby mapping only poetic syllable to continuo, and offers possibilities of coordination with a similar, rhythmic-cycle-free form, the *Viruttam*.

This facet of the decahedral framework links the principles of time and forward motion of poetry in the Monteverdian approach to Karnatik music, opening yet another register of address for hybridity.

Instrumentation.

Stubbs (1994) and Lawrence-King (2014) present insights into the foundational instruments for continuo in *L'Orfeo*, in discussing organ, chittarone, theorbo, and harp. By interpreting the earlier score of *L'Orfeo* (Monteverdi, 1615), later scholarly editions (Monteverdi 1609/1968; 1609/1993; 1609/2016), and a selection from the vast body of extant recordings (Monteverdi & Gardiner, 1990; Monteverdi & Harnoncourt, 1992; Monteverdi & Medlam, 1984; Monteverdi & Savall, 2003), I evaluate my options for continuo instruments in my hybrid creations. However, I hold practical constraints at the forefront; the availability and willingness of a harpsichordist or a lutenist for my project would ideally determine my choice of instrument.

In the Karnatik tradition, each verse of the *Viruttam* is usually followed by a violin response in the same raga. This may be analogised with the inter-verse *ritornello*. In co-creation with Monteverdi, a combination of Indian and Baroque instruments, such as the flute, Baroque violin, and the *Veena*, could be used in realising *ritornelli,* as demonstrated in *Orfeo in India* (Lakerveld, 2011).

Stubbs (1994) elaborates on Agostino Agazzari's (1607) concept of the foundational and the ornamental instruments of the time. A practical application of his discussion is seen in the *L'Orfeo* recording (2008) that he directs.

> In performing Italian music of the early 17th century, the modern interpreter must often answer the question, 'which instrument or combination of instruments should realize the bass?' . . . the score of Monteverdi's *Orfeo* gives us a series of indications for the changing orchestration of the bass in a specific musical context. (Stubbs, 1994, p. 86)

Changing the instrumentation to conform with the singer's emotions and conceits is an approach taken by Monteverdi in the score of *L'Orfeo*; nine continuo markings out of the twenty-two pertain to Orfeo's role. This opens up possibilities for identifying instruments from both traditions that might suitably support the emotions conveyed.

The resonances between the timbral quality of the harpsichord, lute, and the Karnatik plucked instrument, the *Veena*, present possibilities for integrating Karnatik *gamaka* with these instruments (Krishnaswami, 2017). There is much literature relating to the journey of the violin from the West into becoming the instrument of choice for accompanying the voice in Karnatik music (Swift, 1990; Weidman, 2006). The ability of the violin to invoke *gamaka* with continuity and dependability has rendered it indispensable for Karnatik vocal accompaniment and for vocal accompaniment in this research.

The function and potential of musical instruments in realising the structure of the musical declamation, across Monteverdian and Karnatik styles, is explored as a possible tool in hybridity through the aforementioned facet of the decahedral framework.

Ornamentation

The thread of ornamentation runs strongly throughout the discussions on stylistic features of the declamatory form, and yokes composition to performance and composer to performer, as Haynes & Burgess (2016, pp. 154–158) elaborate. I have comparatively discussed and practically problematised vocal ornamentation in Karnatik music and in early opera using *Possente Spirto* as my lens in the ensuing Section. For now, I introduce the key dimensions across which ornamentation influences the hybridity.

The substantive presence of matters related to the voice and ornamentation in Monteverdi's *lettere* indicate that the potential of the voice to move feelings was of importance to Monteverdi. I examined Monteverdi's *lettere* closely (Stevens, 1985, pp. 60–88) and could extrapolate around ten recurrent themes that emerged in the context of singers of the time (both church and chamber). Several of these themes pertain to ornamentation and the ability to improvise. I list them below in an order that approximately reflects the level of importance that Monteverdi gives to each of these attributes in a singer:

1. Trillo
2. Gorgie
3. Clarity in text enunciation
4. Flexibility of voice
5. Awareness of the distinct amplitude levels necessary for chamber and chapel settings
6. Ability to move passions
7. Acting ability
8. Ability to singing securely

9. Ability to compose (he linked this to dependability)
10. Memory

From this collection, I construe that the singer's capability to execute and apply ornaments was highly valued by Monteverdi and linked the virtuosic freedom of the singer to the demands of a text-led approach. This trajectory of thought may be mapped to the 'strength and resourcefulness to adapt to any musical direction' that a Karnatik musician is known to possess (Bailey, 1992, p. 4; Nettl, 2009, pp. 42–43). I compare *gorgie* with its Karnatik proximate, *brigha*, in some detail in Section 4 as my primary case study. A *trillo* or *gorgie* when experienced by my body could map across to Karnatik ornaments; only practice shall reveal this in real time.

This facet of the decahedral framework brings ornamentation into sharp focus, identifying its potential as a rich tool in the development of a culturally informed hybrid approach to the Monteverdian style from an Eastern perspective.

Oratione, *Affect, and* Rasa

Richard Widdess (1995, p. 405) links affect, the emotional response elicited by a performer, to *rasa,* by defining the latter in terms of the former; '*rasa*: an aesthetic sentiment, or *affekt* aroused by dramatic performance and perceived by the audience'. There exists a conceptual nexus between the Baroque notion of *affekt* and *rasa,* the sentiment invoked by a raga in the performer and listener. At this intersection resides the important notion of *oratione,* the delivery of musical speech in a manner that moves the onlookers.

The concept of affect, an aesthetic pertaining to music and theatre in the Baroque (Harnoncourt, 1988), was formalised as a term – 'doctrine of the affects' – in the early twentieth century by Hermann Kretzschmar and Arnold Schering (Nagley & Bujić, 2002). Applied to both vocal and instrumental music, this doctrine grew from the ancient theories of rhetoric and oration, particularly the Aristotelian and Ciceronian representations of the Greek and Latin strands of persuasive speech (Buelow, 2001). Arguably, the doctrine refers to the strategy of delivery of text with music in a manner that moves the onlookers. Therefore, an overarching pertinence to aesthetic explains why Widdess (1995) associates *affekt* with the theory of *rasa* in Indian performing arts.

Contextualising affect and *rasa* within *L'Orfeo,* I draw on Calcagno's (2002) commentary of the Monteverdian notion of *oratione.* Calcagno, drawing on several treatises of the time, describes *oratione* as the means for speech to assume beauty in delivery. It was related to vocalising, acting, and moving the onlookers; it pertained to the performer, the performed, and the audience. The term *oratione* was used by Monteverdi's brother Giulio Cesare Monteverdi in the preface to *Scherzi Musicali* (1607) in his statement, 'music should be the servant of *oratione*' (Strunk, 1950, p. 407). Carter (1993b, p. 518) observes that the order of priorities in Monteverdi's compositional style puts *oratione* at the forefront: 'The triumvirate of *oratione, harmonia* and rhythm together made up *melodia*, the art of composition.' These instances of the usage of the term render it pertinent to a compositional style that is performance inflected, as I have argued for in Section 2. Jed Wentz in his doctoral dissertation distinguishes between 'a fluid, natural and affective' performance of French opera and 'a static, stylised and affected performance'. He observes: 'all aspects of a singer's performance (tone color, tempo, gesture, pronunciation etc.) were meant to correspond in an integrated and holistic way (*vérité*) to the affect of the text as it manifested itself in the performer's body on stage' (Wentz, 2010, p. 21). His view regards the performer's voice and text linked through the thread of affect and he argues for a fluidity of tempo in delivering poetry, aligning also with my approach to text-setting and delivery.

Oratione is the performative element that is inextricably linked to composition, as I have observed in relation to Monteverdi's compositional style for opera. This linkage does not confine itself to the interpretation of composition in performance, but overflows into the way in which performative elements dictated composition. As Cyr (2017, p. 123) observes, 'in Baroque music, the performer and composer shared a more equal role in the compositional process'. In the matter of voice and delivery, this sharing translates to dramatic impact.

Rhetoric and *oratione* are interrelated concepts in early opera. Both are related to delivery as Robert Toft's (2014) work on persuasive singing in the seventeenth century comprehensively establishes. The ability of performers to persuade the audience to empathise, using movement of the body, hands, and face, was referred to in rhetoric as *actio* (Haynes & Burgess, 2016, pp. 122–125). It was tied to their great capacity to emote and induce their felt emotions in the audience; a case of *oratione* translating to embodied performance. As Haynes and Burgess note, 'The performer personifies actio, the fifth Office of rhetoric. It is the performer's interpretation of the composer's inventio and dispositio that the audience will hear, and the audience is moved, not by recognizing the potential in the composer's notes but by depending on the performer's sensitivity and competence' (Haynes & Burgess, 2016, p. 122–123).

In his foreword to his *Madrigali guerrieri et amorosi* (1638), Monteverdi articulates his understanding of three key passions and their correspondences with musical expression: 'the principal passions or affectations of our mind . . .

namely anger [*ira*], moderation [*temeprenzio*], and humility or supplication [*supplicatione*]' (Monteverdi, trans. Strunk, 1950, pp. 413–415). These, he mapped onto three musical *genera* that he developed at that time in his writing, namely, the agitated (*concitato*), the moderate (*temperato*), and the soft (*molle*) (Cyr, 2017, pp. 31–36; Hanning, 2011). Later, in 1752, Quantz named seven feelings or moods and mapped them to musical character. Therefore, while feelings have been mapped to melodic material, Monteverdi's cross-referencing pertains to passions and their implications for composition, particularly in relation to rhetorical principles. The *stile concitato,* for instance, is manifest in the agitated speech-like delivery seen in *Il Combattimento* (Hanning, 2011, pp. 265–267).

The matter of affect links to composition through delivery and melodic material, and both these links are achievable by conceptualising the raga-*rasa* nexus in conjunction with *oratione*. This is, arguably, the most interesting link that subsumes almost all other parameters expressed here within itself.

The performative abilities of the singers of the time became key to the realisation of *oratione* in performance. The anonymous manuscript which presented instructions to singer-actors of the time, *Il Corago,* emerged only in 1630. However, singers induced great emotional responses in their audiences long before that, as history establishes (Savage & Sansone, 1989). Virginia Andreini, the first Arianna, came from a theatre background (*commedia dell'arte*), but not all the Italian female singers did. Public performance by women was forbidden in the Papal states, excluding Bologna, until 1798 (Wistreich, 2012, p. 414). Despite such variance in opportunities and performance situations, the singers – male, female, and castrati – of the early modern age were persuasive rhetoricians; apt bearers of *oratione* (Heller, 2003; Toft, 2014).

Karnatik music has long accepted its position as being undramatic, owing to reasons that I have elucidated in the context of *devadasi* performance practice becoming obliterated (in Section 1). The notions of *oratione* and rhetoric are not traditionally prioritised in Karnatik practice. However, there are instances in which persuasive delivery is manifest in a Karnatik paradigm. The traditional piece *Kalinga nardhana thillana,* of the eighteenth-century composer Oothukadu Venkatasubbier, is often delivered using devices of oration by noted singer Aruna Sairam(2015). A dramatic approach to Karnatik declamation can become a trope to approach *oratione* as an aesthetic and meaning-making experience from an intercultural perspective, thereby interrogating the accepted non-dramatic construct.

Oratione is also the link between my present effort and the embodied historical practices of *devadasi*s. It relates to a right to self-assertion and self-representation in performance, and proclaims the right to be heard, seen, and to express. *Oratione* opens up an important dimension of hybridity and is a key facet of the decahedral framework that links emotion, rhetoric, and vocal delivery.

Sprezzatura *and* Sowkhya

Sprezzatura pervaded the notions of 'nobility' in sixteenth-century Italy and made its way into the vocal music of the times. '*Una certa nobile sprezzatura di canto*' – a certain noble negligence of song – was Caccini's way of reconciling his virtuosic singing tastes with the ideals of the Camerata (Fortune, 2001). *Sprezzatura* is a concept that has been discussed on many levels in seventeenth-century music scholarship (Caccini, 1602/2009a, p. 4; Carter, 1987; Järviö, 2006). Caccini (1614/2009b) locates *sprezzatura* within rhythmic freedom in singing in the preface to his work, *Nuove musiche e nuova maniera di scriverle*:

> Sprezzatura is that charm lent to a song by a few 'faulty' eighths or sixteenths various tones, together with those [similar slips] made in the tempo. These relieve song of a certain restricted narrowness and dryness and make it pleasant, free, an airy, just as in common speech eloquence and variety make pleasant and sweet matters being spoken of. (Caccini, trans. Hitchcock, 1614/2009b, p. 3)

Lawrence-King (2015) describes *sprezzatura* as a 'coolness' in carrying oneself while singing; a sense of casualness and ease. *Sprezzatura* was highly regarded in Italian courts following Baldassare Castiglione's (1528/1900) Platonian treatise on the notions of nobility in a courtier's manner, *Il libro del cortegiano*. Pirrotta and Povoledo (1982, p. 246) reads into *sprezzatura* the 'inborn spontaneity and self confidence that must characterise the performance of a perfect courtier', and sees it as the way of achieving 'intangible elements of rhythmic buoyancy and dynamic flexibility beyond the letter of music'. Wistreich (2000, pp. 187–190; 2013) links *sprezzatura* to singing with the judicious, opportune application of ornaments, referred to as *disposizione*.

This brings me to Monteverdi's observation that, while *recitar cantando* requires a composer, *cantar recitando* was highly improvisatory and could be managed by singers themselves (Stevens, 1985, p. 34). His approach underscores all other approaches to *sprezzatura*, and demonstrates a possible linkage between *sprezzatura* and the comparable concept of *sowkhya* in Karnatik music that relates to a sense of freeness. *Sprezzatura* and *sowkhya* both relate to a state of comfort in interpretation, typical of singers of the Baroque as well as of Karnatik music.

Sowkhya is a feeling (*bhava*) and a state of being. One way to define it is as 'an emotive state of repose' (Kartikeyan, Nandakumar & Vishwanath, 2018, p. 59). Overall, it denotes a sense of flexibility, expertise, and self-awareness in singing. In parallel, Järviö (2011) regards *sprezzatura* as the 'cultivated ability to act with seemingly nonchalant mastery', and uses it as a lens to study her phenomenological experience in singing Monteverdi's *recitar cantando*.

Composer Thyagaraja's piece *Intha sowkhya* is a good example of the use of the word *sowkhya* (Mani, 2012). Here, he refers to the '*sowkhya*' that singing the name of Lord Rama elicits, and the compositional style mirrors this aesthetic. Structured as a slow, meandering melody, it is set in the raga *Kapi*, known for its non-traditional *prayogas*, relaxed *bhava*, and surprising turns of foreign notes (*bhashanga swaras*) that beg masterfulness (Viswanathan & Allen, 2004, p. 46).

My engagement with the concept of *sprezzatura* will stem from my understanding of the related attitude of *sowkhya*, informing a facet of the decahedral framework.

Summation

This framework draws on theory, literature, and aspects of Karnatik practice to develop a conceptual framework for hybridity and interrogation to evolve.

Table A1 in Appendix A summarises some of the specific findings on the convergences and divergences between the two musical practices. These insights have emerged from the application of the decahedral framework, as it relates to music theories, performance cultures, and practices.

Based on the overview of Monteverdi's approaches to the various conceptual parameters that I have consolidated in this Section, I infer that Monteverdi may be considered an exemplary artistic researcher; an exceptional rule-breaker who thwarted convention to establish an aesthetic that he believed would best represent the word through music. He was a supporter of vocal virtuosity and dramatic expression in performers, so much so that he modelled his rhetoric on the influence of ornamentation on the text and content. He 'explicitly articulates' his rationale for the 'natural' and 'intuitive' artistic choices that he makes, a key marker that Crispin (2013, p. 47) advances for artistic research. By his own admission, Monteverdi achieved his ideal of natural imitation of human emotion through his 'new style' and 'in practice' rather than from theory (Monteverdi, *lettera* dated 22 October 22, 1633 in Stevens, 1985, p. 85). He may not have delivered his proposed book *Melodia, ovvero Seconda Prattica*, but his objectives are well understood based upon his correspondences and are reflected through his music.

Through this analysis and framework, I have established that alternate ways of being with music induce alternate ways of knowing music. To interrogate the way in which we handle repertoire that is familiar to us, we must sometimes reassemble what we think we know and how we know what we know. From a destabilisation of the ontological premise, new epistemologies are created. There are alternate ways to analytically approach early music and though they may be unfamiliar to the normative Western notions of musicology, it is this very confusion that renders the exercise motivational and transformative. In the next Section, I centralise one of the most powerful dimensions of interaction between Monteverdi's sung-speech form and the Karnatik musico-poetic form – namely, ornamentation. I attempt to unlock newer ways of knowing (epistemologies) by tapping into newer ways of being (ontologies) and 'becoming' (Davidson & Correia, 2001, p. 76).

4 The Powerful Spirit of Ornamentation

In this Section, I delve into *Possente Spirto* to illustrate the orchestration of co-creativity and innovation in historically informed performance through the complementary lenses of musicology, literature, and practice, across two operative levels. Firstly, on a functional level, I identify certain specific Karnatik ornamentation variants (*gamakas*) within the written-in ornamentation detail in *Possente Spirto*. Secondly, I address the notion of ornamentation from an embodied perspective – as movement, emotion, and sound experienced by the whole singing body during delivery. Overall, I use the idiom of Karnatik ornamentation, *gamaka*, as a doorway to Monteverdi's musical intentions and improvisatory invitations. An intercultural experimentation ensues and materialises as a hybridised practice in a shared 'third space' of liminality where creativity can take flight (Bhabha, 2015).

Monteverdi's approach to a certain kind of repetitive ornament articulated at the throat, the *gorgie,* is of holistic musicality, and surpasses the calculated, additive approach to ornamentation that is seen in the works of some of his contemporaries, including dalla Casa, Caccini, and Zacconi (Palisca 1985, p. 131). As Arnold (1985, p. 324) confirms, '[Monteverdi] rarely uses any ornament, or rhythm merely once: he integrates it firmly into the whole melodic pattern and in doing so differs from most composers of the time.' By comparison, an integrative approach to ornamentation resonates with the Karnatik idea of embellishment that begins at the *gamaka* level and propagates across the entirety of the melodic construct (*prayoga* and *sanchara*), whether composed or improvised (Pearson, 2016). Karnatik *gamaka* is never additive, it is inseparable from the musical contour. Rather, without it, a phrase would not be a raga, it would be a scalar segment (Mani, 2018a). I compare *gorgie* with its Karnatik proximate, *brigha*, is some detail in the ensuing sections.

Scholars have attributed the failure of Orfeo as an orator to the profusion of ornamentation in *Possente Spirto*. As noted to earlier, Monteverdi's deliberate engagement with the middle style level of rhetoric (*delectare*) results in a loss of such content-related gravity. Turning to Karnatik music, ornamentation is a way of life as it was in the Baroque, however, it is never used as a trope for rhetorical intent. Monteverdi's approach to ornamentation extends beyond the purely technical well into the domain of the human and emotional, and in this way, differs markedly from the Karnatik, wherein ornaments are seen primarily as contingent to the raga grammar, the Karnatik sonic aesthetic, and devotion expressed for the 'godly'.

What is interesting in *Possente Spirto* is that Monteverdi *chooses* to render this piece rhetorically unconvincing by his deliberate and overt use of ornaments. That Orfeo, ever the virtuosic singer, fails to be a convincing orator, is conveyed admirably. Orfeo's handling of the many varieties of ornaments is emblematic of grandiloquence (Schwindt, 2014, pp. 240–242). In the Karnatik, by comparison, a singer's rhetorical prowess is measured in terms of their command over ornamentation. Despite variance in the intent of ornamentation across Karnatik music and that of the Baroque, the notion of ornamentation is one of the most interesting points of resonance between these two musical practices.

I believed at the outset of my examination of *Possente Spirto* that a *trillo* or *gorgie* when experienced by my body could map across to Karnatik ornaments – only practice, referenced against theory from both genres and the literature, revealed the path to such an experience in real time. Regarding ornamentation as device to induce emotion resonates with theories of embodied cognition relating to ways in which the body perceives music. These approaches are gaining momentum in musicological discourses of the present. As Godøy (2017, p. 12) notes, 'An essential feature of embodied cognition is that perception, thinking and understanding are all related to mental simulation of body motion, meaning that we mentally imitate the actions that we believe are the cause of what we perceive or that actively trace one or more features of what we perceive.'

In this Section, I look firstly to theory and literature to expand on the subject of ornamentation. I use my practice, drawing on the framework of hybridity from Section 3, to construct a comparative analysis of voice, delivery, and ornamentation across both cultures. I then conclusively link the *gorgie* in *Possente* to a special type of ornamentation in Karnatik music, the *brigha*. Lastly, to contextualise this practice-based exploration in the broader context of the performance cultures of early opera, I draw on critiques of voice in early music. In the light of certain problematic issues faced by vocal performers and pedagogues in the matter of learning and performing the special kind of ornament crucial to seventeenth century vocal practice, the *gorgie*, I argue that there is value in intercultural hybridity. Approaches to pre-romantic voice from a non-Western perspective could revitalise historical vocal technique research and practice in the West.

Surface-Level Comparisons of the Karnatik and Pre-Romantic Voice

Physiognomically, the voice in Karnatik music resonates with the pre-romantic voice on several levels. I draw on the extensive scholarship from vocal peda-gogue/researcher Richard Wistreich on voice and ornamentation in Monteverdi's music to deepen the context of pre-romantic voice here. Wistreich (2000, p. 180) observes of historical practices of early modern singing that, 'singers raised their larynx as the tone became higher, rather than consciously lowering it as in modern classical technique', thus declaring the fundamental difference between pre-romantic singing and the modern technique in opera singing. He attributes this difference to the singing methods that emerged in the late eighteenth century. As described in Garcia's (1847/1984) treatise, the famous technique of depressing the larynx in the upper ends of vocal registers enhanced the carrying power of the voice, and larger opera houses could thus be filled sonically. This development, scholars note, has altered the way singing has been taught and practised since, rendering approaches to the earlier sixteenth- and seventeenth-century voices primarily historical-source based (Potter & Sorrell, 2012, p. 91; Wistreich, 2000, pp. 178–191).

Turning to such sources, I begin my initial comparison of the pre-romantic voice with the Karnatik voice with Marin Mersenne (1636), whose research confirmed that in pre-romantic vocal technique the larynx rose when pitches moved higher, and fell when they moved lower. This observation was verified through pedagogy, in 1755, by Antoine Bérard. Turning to Karnatik voice, the larynx operates in a manner that is similar to that described as normative in pre-romantic singing. It moves up as pitches increase and vice versa. My personal experience is that this is the only way the Karnatik style of singing can ever be realised. Practical examples of current Karnatik practice to testify to this fact (Jaya TV, 2018).

Changing the key centre of a piece to suit the singers' voice such that the chest register came through, without strain, was common practice in the six-teenth and seventeenth centuries, as Caccini's (1602/2009a) preface clearly indicates, and Praetorius (1619) confirms. So also, in Karnatik singing, the tonic for any concert remains fixed throughout and is selected entirely based on the preference of the vocalist on the day. As Durga (1983, p. 3) notes, the ancient treatise *Narada Siksha* (Vedic scripture dating around 2,500 years ago) advises the singer to use chest voice in a comfortable pitch and cautions against the use of falsetto.

In the pre-romantic context, a voice close to the speaking voice was considered, 'more perfect, more noble and more generous' (Wistreich 2000, p. 180, citing Maffei, 1562), lending itself to smaller chamber settings. Giovanni Bardi's recommendations: 'while singing you will behave in a seemly way, so similar to your normal [speaking] manner ...' resonate the same ideal (trans. Palisca 1989, pp. 128–129). Turning to Karnatik music, the pitches are closer to speaking tone. Chamber concerts were the norm in the pre-microphone era of Karnatik music, and when larger halls did come into being in the post-nationalist era the microphone was adopted. While the microphone in Karnatik music has had its supporters and opponents, the positive aspect of it was that the quality of the Karnatik voice that rendered it close to a singer's speaking dynamic range could remain intact (Higgins 1976; Weidman 2001, pp. 112–116). This has meant greater clarity of delicate ornaments and subtleties over larger spaces in Karnatik vocal practice.

Delicacy and subtleties were important features of sixteenth-century chamber singing. Zarlino (1588/1968, p. 253) notes, 'in private rooms one sings with a lower and gentler voice, without shouting'. Amplification in Karnatik voice had eliminated the need for a pronounced alteration in vocal technique of the past when larger halls came into the picture, around the 1940s. However, in the West, this was not the case. Opera houses had to be filled and vocal techniques had to be accordingly reworked in the nineteenth century. The pre-romantic subtle ornate style, therefore, aligns with the Karnatik chamber-music style of voice production.

Other similarities between Karnatik voice and the pre-romantic voice include the absence of vowel modification in both traditions, the ability to hold long tones on pure vowels (known as *fermo* in the West and *karvai* in Karnatik singing), and an unforced tone. A lecture demonstration (Carnaticworld 2016) published by leading scholars of Karnatik music on voice culture demonstrates several of these features, and it is noteworthy that the performers' spoken and singing voices have similar dynamic ranges. My lecture-demonstration series on ragas is a personal example of these aspects (Mani, 2011). The most striking feature that links the pre-romantic voice to the Karnatik voice, however, is ornamentation.

Delving Deeper: Juxtapositions of Ornamentation Varieties

The key feature of Karnatik raga is the connectedness between its pitch positions which is facilitated by microtonal embellishments (*gamakas*) that hook one *swara* to another. *Gamakas* involve a variety of movement-based relationships between pitch positions – whether consecutive, separated by larger intervals, or involving one or more pitches (Viswanathan, 1977, pp. 30–32). The realisation of any melodic line in a Karnatik vocal style is next to impossible without a *gamaka* of some kind embedded in it (Pesch, 1999, p. 73).

Gamakas, as a concept, date back to the *Natyasastra* period (they were called *alankara*, literally meaning adornments), and have evolved through treatises such as *Sangitaratnakara* (thirteenth century) of Sargnadeva, Somanatha's *Ragavibodha* (1609), and *Mahabharata Cudamani* (eighteenth and nineteenth centuries) to their present form (Pesch, 1999, pp. 72–76). *Gamakas* in current performance practice derive from a more recent (1904) treatise of Subbarama Dikshitar, *Sangita Sampradaya Pradarshini* (SSP). SSP discusses fifteen different varieties of *gamakas* and groups them under ten classifications, with symbols (Jayalakshmi, 2002).

Gamakas in current practice (and in SSP) are broadly of three varieties: shakes (*kampita* and related others), stresses (*janta* and related others), and slides (*jaaru*), and may involve one or more *swaras* (Krishna & Ishwar, 2012 p. 14; Pesch, 1999, pp. 74–75). In the context of voice, *gamakas* are a key link between vocal movement, *bhava* (feelings), and bodily gesture (Mani, 2019b; Pearson, 2016). Of the three variants in *gamaka* types, the reiterative stresses are particularly relevant to the written-in ornaments in the *Possente Spirto* vocal line. I have tabulated certain key Karnatik *gamakas* types of Karnatik music that are relevant to this discourse, in Table 4.1.

Turning to seventeenth-century Western ornamentation, the history of embellished solo song in Italy lends context to the kind of ornaments that Monteverdi and his contemporaries employed. Treatises on singing and voice such as those of Zarlino (1558/1968), Vicentino (1555/1996), Maffei (1562/ 1979), Rognoni (1620/2007), and dalla Casa (1584/1989) proliferated from mid-sixteenth-century onwards and carried information on ornamentation. However, it was Caccini's (1602/2009a) publication with an introduction and instructions on specific ornaments of the prevailing culture, *Le Nuove Musiche*, that became a landmark treatise with respect to ornamentation. Caccini's work, alongside Bovicelli's (1594) *Regole*, brought the erstwhile improvised ornaments into the written-in realm of composition (Carter, 1984, p. 209).

These informants, along with the scores, are the key connection early music singers of the present have to their vocal history (Wistreich & Potter, 2013). By contrast, the oral tradition of *guru-sishya parampara* (handing down of knowledge from teacher to student) through which Karnatik music is taught, has enabled the Karnatik vocal techniques to propagate into the present as living

Table 4.1 *Gamaka* types in Karnatik music relevant to *Possente Spirto*

Gamaka	Description
Janta (Stress)	Repeated stresses on a note. More than one note can be involved in a *varisai* – 'string' of janta.
Sphurita (Reiterative)	Starting from note above descending to note below with repeated stresses.
Odukkal (Reiterative)	Quick movement from one note to the next and back.
Orikkai (Reiterative + Slide)	Jumping movement from a swara to the next higher, and descending to the note immediately lower to the start.
Brigha/gorgie (Fast collective)	A collective of various reiterative ornaments assembled as long fast passages, delivered delicately.
Kampita (Oscillation)	A note is presented as an oscillation (may be slight or pronounced), between the notes before and after it.
Jaaru (Slide)	Sliding movement between notes.

oral performance culture. As Neil Sorrell observes, historically informed performance might be 'redundant' in Karnatik music: 'Performers [of Indian classical music] can be oblivious to concerns such as historically informed performance because the conscientiousness of the oral tradition, sustained by the *guru-sishya parampara* makes the concept redundant . . . they will not be led to think that their tradition was in any way disrupted' (Potter & Sorrell, 2012, p. 160). This might explain some of the closeness that Karnatik music demonstrates to the pre-romantic voice. They both hold dear their allegiance to their respective oral traditions of singing.

In the context of early music ornamentation, the popular ornaments of the time are listed in Caccini (1602/2009a) and Rognoni (1620/2007). While the ornaments as well as their terminologies have changed over the centuries, the key varieties are those that involve a reiteration of a note or notes, often with acceleration, and of equal or unequal rhythmic divisions, culminating as pulsations. Many of the ornaments of reiteration of the time find place in Monteverdi's *Possente*. They mainly include the *trillo* (reiteration of a single note), *gruppo* (a two-note trill with a final turn), *ribattuta di gola* (a main-note trill on a long-short dotted rhythm), *tremolo* (a continuous tremble in the voice), and *cascata* (quick descent in scale) (Wistreich 2000, pp. 187–190).

Progressing into the Micro Level: *Brigha* and *Gorgie*

Wistreich (2013, p. 140), links the Monteverdian *gorgie* with the *trillo* in his essay on the migration on the Italian *trillo* to other parts of Europe, telling us, 'The 16th and early seventeenth-century Italian name for the vocal technique of which the *trillo* forms the apogee, is *cantar di gorgia*.' The *gorgie* was sung using a technique called the *cantar di gorgia* (singing of the throat), and was considered the acme of Italian sophisticated singing in the seventeenth century (Wistreich, 2013, pp. 140–142). A comparable ornamentation style, *brigha*, in Karnatik music, takes *gamakas* of a repeated stress variety to a level of continuity, speed, and stylish ease (Terada, 1996, pp. 930–932). Thus, both *gorgie* and *brigha* styles derive from ornaments of reiteration; *gorgie* on the *trillo*, and *brigha* on the *janta* (and the related *sphurita*). In both *brigha* and *gorgie*, the place of a single long note is taken by several divisions, as diminutions. These may be in the same pitch position or across several positions (as *gorgie passaggi*).

The *gorgie*, from the perspective of vocal function, is realised by the rapid opening and closing of the glottis, through a patterned regulation of such a movement. The diminutions of equal or unequal note value render the *gorgie* or *brigha* as not only elements of melody but also of rhythmic syncopation. The *brigha sangatis* (passages) are usually long, comparable to the typical *gorgie passaggi*, testing the limits of breath power, precision, and vocal agility in a singer (Terada, 2000; T. R. Subramaniam, 1985). See my demonstration of *brigha* in Karnatik raga with comparable phrasings from *Possente Spirto* in Videos 4.1 and 4.2. The appearance and sounding of *brigha*, as these recordings evidence, is entirely relatable to the researched literature on the *gorgie*.

The interpretive freedom that the *brigha* offers a singer of Karnatik music may be gathered from Terada (1996, pp. 930–932; 2000, pp. 472–473). His discussion on the *brigha* particularly pertains to *nagaswaram vidwan*, T. N. Rajaratnam Pillai's technique, and its correspondences to an ornate vocal style. In the *nagaswaram*, an ancient reeded wind instrument, the distinct divisions of *brigha* are generated by tonguing. Rognoni (1620/2007), in *Selva*, interestingly notes a similar connection between *gorgie* singing and the tonguing technique used by cornetto players. The *brigha* in Karnatik vocal practice became emblematic of vocal virtuosity, agility, and genius, as the singing of artists including G. N. Balasubramaniam and T. N. Seshagopalan testify (Seshagopalan, 1983, p. 35; T. R. Subramaniam, 1985, p. 75). Likewise, vocal *disposizione,* the descriptive of a singer's ability to use *gorgie*, was linked to 'noble singing' (Wistreich, 2000, pp. 187–190).

Video 4.1 Exploring gorgie ornamentation in Possente Spirto. Video available in online formats.

Two traditional varieties of *gamakas*, the *janta* (repeated stresses on a single note or multiple notes) and *sphurita* (touching the higher note and descending to the lower, stressing final note again), form the primary units that constitute the *brigha*. Another name for the *brigha* is *rava jathi*, literally meaning the free-flowing coarse grains of semolina – the notion of freeness fulfilled by the sustained breath-power, and the coarseness lending to distinction between each grain. The *brigha* is always improvised by the Karnatik singer and realised differently each time in performance or practice sessions. However, the basic material that a performer works with in *brigha* is drawn from a selection of passages in the raga and delivered in a technique learnt from a guru, characteristically by imitation (Schippers, 2007, pp. 120–123).

I now turn to *gorgie*. While written-in *gorgie* were common in early seventeenth-century monody, the improvised addition of ornaments over and above

Video 4.2 Appearance of Karnatik raga during practice-based research into
Possente Spirto. Video available in online formats.

what was on paper was a common practice in singers (Carter, 1984, p. 209). Further, imitation was historically considered a suitable method for learning, as Wistreich notes: '[S]everal sources which try to describe the technique in print confess that it can only really be learned by imitating someone who can demonstrate it' (Wistreich, 2000, p. 188).

Wistreich (email communication with author, 15 January 2017) shared some interesting information on his perceptions of *gorgie* in relation to Indian classical vocal technique with me. He noted that it was tenor Nigel Rogers who had pointed out to him the similarities in laryngeal function between certain vocal techniques of Indian classical music and the *gorgie*. He went on to observe that in developing his fine *gorgie* technique during the 1960s, Rogers had listened to several recordings of Indian classical singers. It was refreshing to note that in a recent talk on historical vocal technique to students, Wistreich had played a *Behag* raga recording of Ajoy Chakraborthy (a well-known singer of the North Indian classical tradition) preceding Nigel Rogers' recording of a Francesco Rasi madrigal, to illustrate the striking similarities in their *gorgie* style.

Physiognomically, the *brigha* derives its power from the lungs, however, the regulation of this power into light, agile sound by slicing it into minute divisions that 'roll' through the voice is achieved in the larynx through the rapid articulation of vocal folds. Venkatraman (1984) and T. R. Subramaniam (1985) describe the sonic manifestation of this articulation in the context of the great *vidwan* G. N. Balasubramaniam (GNB), known for his *brigha* style. Several recordings of GNB (Indian Record Manufacturing Company [INRECO] 2014) align closely, in my mind, with the description of *gorgie* that Wistreich advances, following a detailed discussion relating to Monteverdi's letters on voice:

> Any discussion or, more importantly, practice of vocal articulation must begin with the simple acknowledgement that *gorgie* are articulated in the throat by a rapid closing and opening of the glottis. There is no possibility of making true *gorgie* with 'diaphragm articulation'. But the sound has to be generated and projected [by the breath from lungs], as well as articulated. (Wistreich, 1994, p. 15).

The *gorgie* was frequently discussed by Monteverdi, particularly in his letters evaluating singers' abilities. In the letter cited here, for instance, he appraises a singer from a 'what not to do when singing *gorgie*' perspective, going on to recommend best practice:

> Regarding the ornaments (*gorgie*), he does not separate them too well because he fails most of the time to join the chest voice to the middle (throat) voice, for if the middle (throat) fails the chest voice, the ornamentation becomes harsh, hard and offensive; if the chest voice fails that of the throat, the ornamentation (*gorgie*) becomes unctuous, as it were, and almost continuous in the voice, but when both function, the ornamentation (*gorgie*) comes off both sweetly and separated, this is most natural. (Monteverdi, *lettera* dated 24 July 1627 in Stevens, 1985, p. 101)

Wistreich (1994, p. 14) clarifies that the middle voice (*voce di gola*) in this translation pertains to the site of articulation of the *gorgie*, the throat. The *gorgie* derives its power from the chest voice, referred to as the *voce di petto,* in this context. The middle/chest references in Monteverdi's letter are notably different from the modern-day use of the terms (from a vocal register perspective).

Wistreich and Monteverdi's descriptions of *gorgie* invoked gestural memories of the *brigha* in me, in line with embodied cognition theories (see, for instance, the work of Godøy, 2017, p. 12). Above and beyond the theoretical similarities, the bodily resonance that I had with the *gorgie* concept became my 'ground zero' (Husserl 1907/2001), as this journal entry shows: 'As I scan through every word: about the chest supporting the throat, and glottal closures, I am feeling the excitement. My body is pre-reflectively telling me that it has experienced this sensation many times. A familiar friend. A part of my singing being' (27 August 2017).

Experiencing the Comparisons through Practical Experimentation

One of the greatest advantages of being a performer-researcher working in a transcultural musical scenario is that the theories from extant literature, the communicated experiences of others, and encrusted impressions from one's own practice arising out of one's earlier interactions with the world, can all be put through an additional layer of scrutiny through practical experimentation within one's current space.

Accordingly, prior to embarking on the experimental/reflective sessions focused on ornamentation, I referred to versions of *Possente Spirto* from several tenors to inform myself about ways in which singers have interpreted the theories of *gorgie* in their practice. I identified resonances with certain renditions, particularly Nigel Rogers (Monteverdi & Medlam, 1984), Anthony Rolfe Johnson (Monteverdi & Gardiner, 1990), and Nicolas Achten (Scherzi Musicali, 2014). When I listened to Nigel Rogers' *Possente Spirto* for the first time, I jumped with joy. His *gorgie* reminded me so much of GNB's *brigha*-laden singing style (INRECO, 2014). As I listened to it repetitively, I sensed Damasio's (1994) *body-minded brain* at work in me, and journaled: 'As I hear him sing gorgie, my vocal folds experience a 'mirroring' ... I sense a familiarity. My body acknowledges this knowing. I recognise this sensation. This seems really close to what I have been singing as brigha, all these years' (3 August 2017).

I revisited embodied cognition theories to help me understand why and how I identified with Monteverdian ornaments, the *gorgie*, in particular. A relevant embodied approach is expressed by Arnie Cox (2001, 2011) who defines 'mimetic hypothesis' as our understanding of music through 'tacit imitation' or 'mimetic participation'. This understanding, he notes, is based on our prior doing of the acts and embedded embodied experiences of similar sound production (Cox, 2001, p. 195). This, I believe, explains why I immediately identified with the *gorgie* sung by Nigel Rogers. This resonance with my sense of identification came about because, as explained by mimetic hypothesis, hearing Nigel's *gorgie* and looking at the score aligned, for me, with a bodily action that I had profoundly experienced as an intrinsic part of my singerly experience, the *brigha* vocalisation. As Cox (2011, para. 24) confirms, 'the ability to imagine performing an action is informed by experiences of actually performing that action, and the more experience one has performing a specific action, the more vivid and accurate the imagination is likely to be.'

I extended this discourse to a reading of texts and looking at images of scores as well. As Hunter (2013, p. 167) notes of embodied cognition, 'this subjective imaginative experience, our sense of ourselves, our thought, our mind, is inextricably bound to brain and body'.

I adopted a reflective practice approach to experiencing the ornamentation. I drew on the reflective musicianship approach of AustbØ et al. (2015) in considering the words, singing the ornaments as per the score, reflecting on the act and sound, deriving insights from what I felt as I sang, and reimagining *gamakas*, into practice.

Embodying the Ornate

Vocality has been directly linked to sexuality, and Bonnie Gordon (2004) situates ornamentation squarely within her feminist critique of virtuosic singing in the early Baroque. She evaluates the 'beating throat, active lips and tongues' discussed in singing treatises in the context of writings on ancient gynaecology, such as those of Galen, and notes that ornamental eloquence in women was considered as another form of incontinence; a leakage of excesses, through the throat (Gordon, 2004, p. 31). She clearly observes that, 'articulated in the throat, *gorgia* induced the rapid closing and opening of the glottis, an action paralleled to the opening of the uterus imagined to accompany orgasm'. While the Orphic ornamental eloquence in *Possente* has been deemed overt and grandiloquent, a similar display by a woman would have been deemed as an act of unbridled sexuality in those times, as Heller (2003, p. 48–52) affirms.

Interestingly, *brigha* in Karnatik music has been associated with the masculine. The exception was M. L. Vasanthakumari who propagated the *brigha* style in female voices (Nayak, 2000, p. 173). In my past, while singing Karnatik *kacceris*, I had always privileged mind over body. I would conceive *brigha* in my mind, as a technicality, and sing it. Perhaps I was trained thus – to discount the participation of the body in the *brigha* process lest it rendered me provocative.

In my reflective sessions, I realised that I was initiating the ornament from bodily experience. I allowed my body to be the first receiver, and the agency that pre-empted the impending *gamaka*. The act of singing legitimised those affinities that I had experienced upon initially perceiving the *gorgie*. As posited by Merleau-Ponty (1945/1993), bodily understanding is pre-reflective and prefigures any intellectual processing. The body as crucial to cognitive activity: the 'centre for all knowledge and experience', 'the privileged ontological' (Waskul & Vannini, 2006, p. 8) came forth as experienced realities.

This journal entry made after one of the reflective sessions reveals my state of mind at the time:

> I am holding onto the embodied passion tighter than to the cerebral knowledge of the notes. I think only about the word and the ornateness embedded within. The gorgie is Orfeo's ornamented cry. He is singing . . . to convey his desperation. He knows nothing else, he is a singer. A singer who communicates through ornament. Caronte does not see this feeling, he only sees a show-off. (10 August 2017).

I engaged in these reflective sessions on ornamentation in June 2017. One session was particularly fulfilling for me and revealed many instances of commonality between my vocal style, *gamakas*, the text, and the Monteverdian ornaments, and heavily drew on the framework of hybridity outlined in the previous Section. I annotated this video clip with descriptive and reflective comments, and embedded relevant sections from the 1615 edition of the score of *L'Orfeo* within it (Monteverdi, 1615). I made this session publicly available on YouTube (Mani, 2018b), and this is discussed in Mani (2019b; 2019c).

At the completion of this stage, I had acquired insights into ornamentation in the context of the melodic figures in *Possente*, and an overall idea of the application of *gamakas*, in general, to certain ornaments typical of Monteverdi and the times. I had not yet consciously situated the melodic lines in relation to ragas. However, this identification, I can say retrospectively, had intuitively begun at this point. *Gamaka* variants, both as 'ornamental note and a type of short decorative phrase' which are 'an integral part of a particular raga', surfaced in the experimentations with ornaments here, opening out raga possibilities for *Possente Spirto* (Pesch, 1999, p. 73).

Based on my impressions from the practice sessions, I have mapped certain ornaments of reiteration that appear in *Possente Spirto* to specific *gamakas* from Table 4.1, as Figures 4.1 and 4.2 show. *Kampita* occurred across most phrases, and is a key marker of Karnaticisation, described in Krishna and Ishwar (2012, p. 14) as 'the sound of Karnatak music aesthetic' and by Pesch (1999, p. 74) in two different ways – as subtle vibrato-like oscillations, and as more pronounced

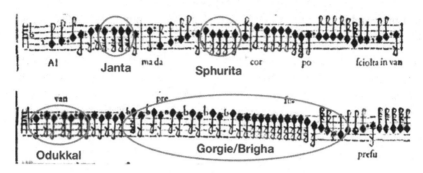

Figure 4.1 Certain *gamakas* mapped onto *Possente Spirto*, score sample 1 (Monteverdi, 1615, pp. 53–54)

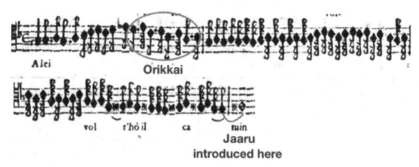

Figure 4.2 Certain *gamakas* mapped onto the *Possente Spirto*, score sample 2 (Monteverdi, 1615, p. 58)

oscillations. The *Jaaru*, like a glissando, surfaced in practice in a few key moments as Figure 4.2 indicates and the media pointer at '*il cammin*' (8:21) demonstrates. As the annotations in the Media file Reflective Transcultural Ornamentation explain, the ornaments in *Possente* and their expressive qualities map to the text and emotion and are bolstered when sung with *gamaka* touches and embodied involvement. Since I have engaged with detailed annotation in the media, I refrain from analysing this particular reflective session in-text, at any length.

The resonance that I experienced with *gorgie* demonstrates that singing traditions that are seemingly disparate may indeed have correspondences that practice can illuminate. Further, these correspondences could shape one another in the present.

Over the next Section, I discuss the relevance of my hybrid vocal approach to the performance culture of early opera and to a reconsideration of Western music from a historically global perspective.

5 Reimagination: Critiques, Opportunities, Conclusions

Current Western scholars of voice are (sometimes painfully) aware that it is the treatises, the descriptive accounts of singing, the scores, analyses, and the extant recordings that inform their understanding of the historical vocal technique of the seventeenth century, across performative and pedagogical contexts (Wistreich & Potter, 2013). Following Garcia's (1847/1984) manual, there came a change in opera singing styles. Large opera houses had to be filled with sound, and new techniques were developed accordingly; the divide between the later vocal styles and the pre-romantic styles became more pronounced. Today's singers and pedagogues of early music, therefore, contend with the reality that what seventeenth-century singers may have actually 'sounded' like is unknown. 'We can only speculate about what the singers actually did', notes Potter in his essay on historical voices (Potter & Sorrell, 2012, p. 70). As Haynes (2007) observes, making music in the present by drawing on aspects of it from the past is one effective way to reconcile with such speculation: 'What is considered verifiable history – almost never offers a complete picture; in the case of music, not even recordings (if they existed) could do that. Performers have to fill in that picture and transform it into coherent music' (p. 28).

The early musical revival of the 1960s and 1970s ushered in a wave of recordings that became popular and established a certain kind of normative early music vocal sound. This movement claimed to have 'authentically' reconstructed the past (Upton 2012; Wilson 2013). In the 1980s and 1990s influential scholars including Taruskin (1982, 1988, 1995), and Dreyfus (1983) argued that this movement's claims to authenticity were 'pretentious' and that they were yet another strand of musical modernism typical of the twentieth century whose agenda was 'shocking complacent ears with new sounds' (Lindenberger, 1998, p. 47). Through the next few decades, researched, historically informed performances proliferated, and now testify to the agenda foreseen by Taruskin (1995, p. 4) as 'not the truth, but taste' being 'on the march'. Since then, the term authenticity has been confined within the closed doors of 'scare quotes' (Taruskin, 1995, p. 4).

What the seventeenth-century voice sounded like is now less important than how our present capacities may be combined with history, using research, to produce music of the past, for and in the present. From a performer's point of view, I propose that one does not need an excuse to adopt an approach other than the normative to singing Monteverdi. Pushing boundaries in the course of artmaking is a given; this has indeed marked early music revival, as the emergence of successful 'non-normative vocal styles' and 'experimental' approaches of Janita Noorman, Andrea von Ramm, Cathy Berberian, and even Nigel Rogers, testify (Upton 2012, para. 14). Further, the history of early modern Europe shows that cultural plurality and global mobility prevailed and influenced the arts and cultures of the time (Heller, 2014). Approaches to the music of the period from Eastern perspectives, such as my own, reimagine the rich cultural histories in the present. Decolonising Western music practice and musicology goes hand in hand with respecting the pluralities of the past. To refer again to Leech-Wilkinson's statement (2017, para. 8), 'old ways of reassuring ourselves that all is well' in early music are questionable in themselves, not least due to the authenticity problems from earlier on.

Taking a cursory glance at the twentieth-century early music revival, Potter summarises this problematic issue with much greater clarity and authority than I can afford, considering my non-Western musical back-ground. He notes, 'there's nothing wrong with the results [of the early music movement] … incidentally, it's just that it's misleading to use a term like 'historically informed'' (Wistreich & Potter, 2013, p. 25). He clarifies that the early music movement of the 1960s and 1970s presented interesting newness. Their vocal sound, however, 'wasn't the product of research (and you won't find any evidence for it in the literature)', Potter notes. Not that it needed to be; the problem was that it claimed to be. The ingrained vocal sound in many of those recordings still holds sway and often renders newer efforts, historically informed or otherwise, more rebellious than they actually are.

Potter converses here with Wistreich in an interesting article on pre-romantic voice; he critiques the origins and discusses the ramifications of the early music movement for the present (Wistreich & Potter, 2013). I quote Potter here at some length to establish my point that newer approaches often face resistances that stem from unfounded premises:

> The truth is we invented the early music vocal sound based on what we wanted it to be like, and on the voices of a small number of singers with particular talents. The small-scale, refined, straight, disciplined early music singing that we were used to came out of nowhere (or perhaps the head of David Munrow!): it wasn't the product of research (and you won't find any evidence for it in the literature). Even when singers began to look at pedagogical sources and so on, they (we) chose to ignore those bits that didn't fit the model we had in our heads. An entire pedagogy was devel-oped by people who claimed to know how 17th- or 18th-century singing was supposed to go, but whose knowledge was based mostly on their own experience of the late 20th-century early music movement, rather than an understanding of the sources. The huge success of early music recordings

then made it impossible to go back and start again. (Potter, in Wistreich & Potter, 2013, p. 25)

Wistreich and Potter (2013) go on to recommend that singers approaching musics of the past, particularly historical vocal technique, take initiative not only by undertaking research based on textual sources, but also by practically exploring their research through experimentation with their voice, using their vocal resources. Studies such as those of Järviö (2006; 2015) and Thomaidis (2013a; 2013b) which explore the embodied 'now' in voice while also considering techniques of the past are notable exemplars that demonstrate this approach. By combining the performative turn in musicology, the phenomenological turn in voice studies, and a drive for newness with a historically informed approach, a picture of history could be reimagined for the present. Hence, Järviö refers to her approach as 'embodied historiography' (UniArts Helsinki, 2018).

Through this research, I have approached Monteverdian repertoire by drawing on theoretical, practical, and historical aspects of the multiple dimensions across which hybridity can ensue, including melody, rhythm, emotion, and effective vocal delivery – this has been a rich and rewarding experience. Drawing on my experiences, I propose that newer perspectives on the early modern voice and musical declamation that are informed by research and supported by practice might benefit the field, offering alternative, fresh, and informed ways to reimagine the pre-romantic voice and repertoire. This model for hybridity, analysis, and practical application of varied approaches to texts from the past, can be regarded as one that is culturally inclusive and historically cognate; not merely rebellious, which it certainly is also.

Conclusions: Reimagined Connections

I conclude with a brief consideration of the aspects of cultural plurality and mobility that marked the history of early modern Europe, for, reimagining early modern music practice and musicology goes hand in hand with respecting the pluralities of the time. Intercultural hybrid approaches to Italian music from that period, such as mine, hold relevance for the rightful representation of the long and varied histories of Western music in the present. Italy in the sixteenth and seventeenth centuries abounded in travellers from the East, and was home to depictions of the 'exotic' in theatrical productions, as Heller (2014, p. 52) notes: 'One of the most intriguing features in all these entertainments [*commedia dell'arte,* and masque] is the attempt to incorporate elements of foreign and exotic cultures. The fascination with the exotic was inspired in no small part by early modern explorers of the East.'

That Monteverdi had both opportunity and the enthusiasm to connect with Eastern traditions of ornamentation may be construed from this excerpt from his letter:

> What I did see in Mantua thirty years ago, played and put together by a certain Arab who had just come from Turkey, was a cittern, the size of ours, strung with the same strings and similarly played, but it had this difference – its belly was half wood around the part near the neck, and half of sheepskin around the underneath part ... the small finger of the quill hand making the said sheepskin dance while he stopped the chord. Those chords came out with a tremolo motion which gave a very pleasing effect. I have heard nothing more novel that was to my liking. (Monteverdi, *lettera* dated 2 February 1634 in Monteverdi & Stevens, 1980, p. 325)

Monteverdi describes what could be imagined as microtonal inflections being enabled on chords; an Eastern sonic world was available to him through such experiences during his active composing years. I certainly do not argue that Monteverdi and his contemporaries were clearly influenced by music from the Eastern cultures, not least Karnatik music, nor is such an argument within the scope of this research. However, it is interesting to consider that such a proposition need not necessarily be an impossibility. The framework of hybridity proposed earlier and this deeper study into ornamentation demonstrate the ways in which convincing alternative approaches to performance practices can indeed emerge from positions and cultures that are normatively marginalised.

It is a certainty that the music of Monteverdi and his contemporaries, including Luzzaschi and Frescobaldi, was born at a time when Europe was at the height of its cultural mobility and migration (Smith & Findlen, 2013), not unlike the world in the present. The cultural situations of early modern Europe have direct implications for present constructs of music research. Today, we are faced with artistic and ethical responsibilities to respond to the manifestations of cultural plurality across histories of global musical practices: indeed, Leach, Fallows, and Van Orden (2015) declare 'a general recognition of the borderless mobility of music and musicians in this period is now gradually undermining the vestiges of 19th-century nation-state musicology' (p. 194). Efforts such my own *brigha* approach to *gorgie* are an example of a recognition of borderless mobility in the music of the present.

The history of ethnic encounters in early modern Europe is a field of scholarship that is gaining traction and testifies to the fact that a global network had developed itself during the sixteenth century in early modern Europe (Betteridge, 2007). Rubiés' (2007) work on travellers' accounts from South India are noteworthy. Horodowich (2005, pp. 1039–1043), in her study of

Venice, notes that music and the allied arts in Europe at that time would have been significantly influenced by the cultural others, especially in the context of Italy. The findings of such scholarship present a convincing picture of the kind of cultural influences that Europe enjoyed at that time, as Van Orden notes in her essay:

> Europe that once ended at the Iron Curtain will now need to include music in Bohemia, Silesia, Moravia, and the Ottoman Empire, and as scholars begin to take stock of the profound multiculturalism of cities like Prague and Rome, I believe we will see more attention paid to the role of vernacular songs in projecting ethnic identity at this time of great cultural mobility. (Leach et al., 2015, p. 217)

Such understandings have led to ground-breaking approaches to the study of the history of Western music from a global perspective. The *Balzan Project: Towards a Global History of Music*, headed by Prof. Reinhardt Strohm at Oxford University is one such. It comprises several case studies which connect the New World, South America, the Mediterranean and Ottoman areas, India, as well as other parts of East Asia, to Europe, and therefore to the history of Western classical music as we now understand it. Interesting intersections, provocations, and invitations for future research have emerged through this project (Balzan Research Project, 2013–17; Strohm, 2018).

Monteverdi Reimagined is the name I gave to my production that ensued from the research reported in this Element (Mani, 2018b). The name refers to both the musical and the cultural constructs being reimagined and recombined for the present. The implications of this critical discussion run deep for research on transcultural and transdisciplinary approaches to music analysis and performance. It offers a critical analysis of early opera in the context of voice and ornamentation, calling out its evidentiary biases and thereby incisively exposing a performer's craft choices in the present. It considers the impact of prevalent discourse and identifies the need to disinvest from the canonical, destabilise the established, and recentre knowledge and assumptions around what constitutes 'correct' knowledge across both cultures. Overall, this discourse holds implications for a decentralised history of Western music, and consequentially, a culturally plural, inclusive, and diverse present for a culture of Western music that is seeking to push boundaries beyond the canon and into a globalised future, now more than ever.

Appendix A

Dimensions of Interaction in Karnatik Music and Early Opera

This table has emerged from the comparative analyses and artmaking processes that have underpinned this research.

Table A1 Dimensions of interaction between Karnatik *Viruttam* and declamation in early opera

DIMENSIONS OF INTERACTION	KARNATIK VIRUTTAM	DECLAMATION IN EARLY OPERA
CONTENT BUILDING & DELIVERY		
Context	Art music, using raga and poetry. Non-representational.	To convey drama to an audience using poetry using music. Representational and referential.
Nature of form	Fully improvised by singer.	Fully composed by composer. Improvisation expected from singer.
Musical organisation	Verse–Violin response–Verse etc.	Strophe–*ritornello*–strophe etc.
Order of priorities	Raga and vocal virtuosity primary. Meaning/pronunciation/word-splitting secondary. Priorities decided by singer.	Wordsetting, meaning, pronunciation primary. Melody secondary. Priorities decided by composer to best serve drama.
Melody and rhythm	Entirely raga based. One or many ragas feature, one after another. No cyclic Tala. *Laya* related metre of poetry.	Modality/Tonality co-exist. Modes change within piece. *Tactus* dictates forward motion. Syllables at interplay with continuo give rise to flexible rhythm.

Table A1 (cont.)

DIMENSIONS OF INTERACTION	KARNATIK VIRUTTAM	DECLAMATION IN EARLY OPERA
Textures	Vocal line leads. Violin follows/responds to voice. No harmonic substrate, except *tanpura* drone.	Voice and continuo combination. Harmony and dissonances jointly constructed by composer.
Text & meaning	Tamil metrical poetry on Hindu Gods. Moric metres.	Italian metrical poetry. Syllabic metres. Dramas from ancient tragedies.
Ornamentation	Highly ornamented. Dependant on singer's *bani* (style absorbed from guru) Raga grammar-led	Ornamentation written-in/improvised. Dependant on rhetorical style, composer's intent and singer's abilities. Text-led.
Voice (dynamic, physiognomy, functionality)	Voice close to spoken tone. Volume limited in vocal projection. Larynx elevates on singing higher. Hence limited range, delicate ornaments, fast *brigha* (equivalent to *gorgie*).	Voice close to spoken tone. Volume limited in vocal projection. Larynx elevates on singing higher. Limited range, delicate ornaments, facile, fast *gorgie.*
Style of delivery	Primarily song-like and ornate. Concept of rhetorical styles not prevalent.	Primarily sung-speech (*recitar cantando*) or sometimes spoken-song (*cantar recitando*) and embellished (*cantar di garbo*)

PERFORMANCE CULTURES		
Emotion	Traditional emotion *bhakti* (devotion). Emotion felt and conveyed mainly through raga, rarely through poetic content. Mainly spiritual, not demonstrative.	Various emotions of life conveyed through wordsetting and embodied delivery strategies. Deliberate and demonstrative.
Gender	Gendered. Demureness expected in female singers.	Gendered. Stereotyping present. Woman's role usually tied to lamenting. *Castrati* popular. All-male performances were held (performers and audience). Female singers were also actors.
Gesture/ Embodiment	Present female performers typically discouraged from using excessive gesture. Historically, hereditary *devadasis* used mimetic and representational gesture and movement in singing. At present, gesture used to indicate raga contour / tempo/ ornamentation etc. and *not to convey textual meaning or drama.*	Hand and facial gesture was rhetorical and normative. Emotionally charged.
Notation cultures	*Viruttam* not notated since fully improvised. Notation, in general, pedagogy-related, not performance.	Notated, not prescriptive. Written to be memorised and interpreted in performance.

Table A1 (cont.)

DIMENSIONS OF INTERACTION	KARNATIK VIRUTTAM	DECLAMATION IN EARLY OPERA
Performance spaces	Historically, courts, temples, and salons, sans amplification (*devadasis*). Present performance spaces usually large halls, with amplification.	No amplification. Chamber performance spaces much smaller compared to opera Houses.
Stage/settings/ costumes	No sets. Elevated singing platform. Seated posture. Traditional South Indian attire (*saree/dhoti*). Visual aspect in performance tied to personality of singer rather than content of music.	Sets and costumes present. Stage machinery common. Attire according to subject matter and character. Visual aspect ties with the aural and story situation.
Society (performers/ audiences)	Mainly monocultural: South Indian *brahmin* community. Casteism present. Sometimes multicultural, specifically fusion contexts, universities abroad, International festivals.	Monocultural at papal states such as Mantua. Culturally plural public in Venezia. Present performers & audiences mainly from Western cultures.

References

Abbate, C. (2004). Music: Drastic or gnostic? *Critical Inquiry, 30*(3), 505–536.

Agazzari, A. (1607). *Del sonare sopra'l basso con tutti li stromenti e dell'uso loro nel conserto* (No. 37). Forni.

Apte, V. S. (1970). *The Student's Sanskrit-English Dictionary: Containing Appendices on Sanskrit Prosody and Important Literary and Geographical Names in the Ancient History of India.* New Delhi: Motilal Banarsidass.

Aristotle. (2014). Politics. In J. Barnes (ed.), *Complete works of Aristotle: Revised Oxford Translation,* Vol. 2). Princeton, NJ: Princeton University Press, pp. 1986–2130.

Arnold, D. (1985). Performing practice. In D. Arnold & N. Fortune, eds., *The New Monteverdi Companion.* London, UK: Faber & Faber, pp. 319–333.

Austbø, H., Crispin, D., & Sjøvaag, J. H. (2015). The reflective musician: Interpretation as co-creative process. *Research Catalogue: An International Database for Artistic Research: Norwegian Artistic Research Programme.* www.researchcatalogue.net/view/86413/86414/0/0.

Bailey, D. (1992). *Improvisation: Its Nature and Practice in Music.* New York: Da Capo Press.

Balzan Research Project. (2013). *Towards a global history of music.* www .music.ox.ac.uk/research/projects/past-projects/balzan-research-project/.

Betteridge, T. (ed.). (2007). *Borders and Travellers in Early Modern Europe.* Burlington, VT: Ashgate.

Bhabha, H. (2015). Foreword. In P. Werbner & T. Moodood, eds., *Debating Cultural Hybridity: Multicultural Identities and the Politics of Anti-Racism.* London, UK: Zed Books, pp. ix–xiii.

Bovicelli, G. B. (1594). *Regole: Passaggi di Musica.* Venice: Giacomo Vincenti.

Buelow, G. J. (2001). Theory of the affects. In S. Sadie & J. Tyrell, eds., *The New Grove Dictionary of Music and Musicians,* 2nd ed. New York: Grove.

Caccini, G. (2009a). *Le Nuove Musiche* (H. W. Hitchcock, trans.), 2nd ed. Middletone, WI: A-R Editions. (Original work published 1602, Florence, Italy: Marescotti).

Caccini, G. (2009b). *Nuove Musiche e Nuova Maniera di Scriverle* (H. W. Hitchcock, trans.), 2nd ed. Middleton, WI: A-R Editions. (Original work published 1614, Florence, Italy: Marescotti).

Calcagno, M. (2002). 'Imitar col canto chi parla': Monteverdi and the creation of a language for musical theater. *Journal of the American Musicological Society, 55*(3), 383–431.

Calcagno, M. (2012). *From Madrigal to Opera: Monteverdi's Staging of the Self.* Berkley, CA: University of California Press.

Carnaticworld. (2016, October 8). *Guidelines to students: Breathing techniques in Carnatic singing* [Video file]. https://youtu.be/hRaNBSpIhyw.

Carter, T. (1984). On the composition and performance of Caccini's 'Le nuove musiche' (1602). *Early Music, 12*(2): 208–217.

Carter, T. (1987). Guilio Caccini (1551–1618): New facts, new music. *Studi Musicali, 16*, 13–31.

Carter, T. (1993a). North Italian courts. In C. Price, ed., *The Early Baroque Era: From the Late 16th Century to the 1660s*. London, UK: MacMillan Press, pp. 23–48.

Carter, T. (1993b). *Possente spirito:* On taming the power of music. *Early Music, 21*(4), 517–523.

Carter, T. (1999). Singing *Orfeo:* On the performers of Monteverdi's first opera. *Recercare, 11*, 75–118.

Carter, T. (2002). *Monteverdi's Musical Theatre.* New Haven, CT: Yale University Press.

Carter, T. (2012). Performance in the sevententh century: An overview. In C. Lawson & R. Stowell, eds., *The Cambridge History of Musical Performance*. Cambridge, UK: Cambridge University Press, pp. 377–398.

Castiglione, B. (1900). *Il Libro del Cortegiano* (T. Hoby, trans., 1561, & W. Raleigh, ed., 1900). London, UK: David Nutt. (Original work published 1528, Venice, Italy: Aldine).

Chafe, E. T. (1992). *Monteverdi's Tonal Language.* New York: Schirmer Books.

Chew, G. (1989). The perfections of modern music: Consecutive fifths and tonal coherence in Monteverdi. *Music Analysis, 8*(3), 247–273.

Coessens, K., Crispin, D., & Douglas, A. (2009). *The Artistic Turn: A Manifesto*. Leuven, Belgium: Leuven University Press.

Cook, N. (2007). *Music, Performance, Meaning: Selected Essays*. Aldershot, UK: Ashgate.

Cook, N. (2015). Performing Research: An institutionalised perspective. In M. Doğantan-Dack, ed., *Artistic Practice as Research in Music: Theory, Criticism, Practice*. Farnham, UK: Ashgate, pp. 23–36.

Cook, N. (2018). *Music as Creative Practice*. New York: Oxford University Press.

Cox, A. (2001). The mimetic hypothesis and embodied musical meaning. *Musicae Scientiae, 5*(2), 195–212.

Cox, A. (2011). Embodying music: Principles of the mimetic hypothesis. *Music Theory Online*, *17*(2). https://mtosmt.org/issues/mto.11.17.2/mto.11.17.2 .cox.html.

Crispin, D. (2013). From territories to transformations: Anton Webern's Piano Variations Op. 27 as a case-study for research in-and-through musical practice. In P. de Assis, W. Brooks & K. Coessens, eds., *Sound and Score: Essays on Sounds, Score and Notation*. Leuven, Belgium: Leuven University Press, pp. 47–60.

Crispin, D. (2015). Artistic research in/as composition: Some case notes. In G. Nierhaus, ed., *Patterns of Intuitions: Musical Creativity in the Light of Algorithmic Composition*. Dordrecht, Netherlands: Springer, pp. 317–327.

Cusick, S. G. (1994). 'There was not one lady who failed to shed a tear': Arianna's lament and the construction of modern womanhood. *Early Music*, *22*(1), 21–44.

Cusick, S. G. (2007). Monteverdi studies and new musicologies. In J. Whenham & R. Wistreich, eds., *The Cambridge Companion to Monteverdi*. Cambridge, UK: Cambridge University Press, pp. 249–260.

Cyr, M. (2017). *Performing Baroque music*. New York: Routledge. (Original work published 1992, Farnham, UK: Ashgate Publishing).

dalla Casa, G. (1989). *Il vero modo di diminuir* (J. Rosenberg, trans.).*Historic Brass Society Journal*, 1(1), 109–114. (Original work published 1584, Venice, Italy: Angelo Gardano).

Damasio, A. R. (1994). *Descartes' Error: Emotion, Reason and the Human Brain*. New York: Grosset/Putnam.

Davidson, J. W. (2015). Practice-based music research: Lessons from a researcher's personal history. In M. Doğantan-Dack, ed., *Artistic Practice as Research in Music: Theory, Criticism, Practice*. Farnham, UK: Ashgate, pp. 81–90.

Davidson, J. W. (2016). Creative collaboration in generating an affective contemporary production of a seventeenth-century opera. In M. S. Barrett, ed., *Collaborative Creative Thought and Practice in Music*. Abingdon, UK: Routledge, pp. 173–186.

Davidson, J. W., & Correia, J. S. (2001). Meaningful musical performance: A bodily experience. *Research Studies in Music Education*, *17*(1), 70–83.

de Goede, T. (2005). From dissonance to note-cluster: The application of musical-rhetorical figures and dissonances to thoroughbass accompaniment of early 17th-century Italian vocal solo music. *Early Music*, *33*(2), 233–250.

Doğantan-Dack, M. (2015). Artistic research in the classical music performance. *PARSE*, *1*, 29–42. https://parsejournal.com/article/artistic-research-in-classical-music-performance/.

Dreyfus, L. (1983). Early music defended against its devotees: A theory of historical performance practice in the twentieth century. *Musical Quarterly*, *69*(3), 297–322.

Durga, S. A. K. (1983). Indian literature on vocal abuse. *Asian Music*, *15*(1), 1–10.

Fabbri, P. (1994). *Monteverdi* (T. Carter, trans.). Cambridge, UK: Cambridge University Press.

Fenlon, I. (1985). The Mantuan stage works. In D. Arnold & N. Fortune, eds., *The New Monteverdi Companion*. London: Faber & Faber, pp. 251–287.

Fenlon, I. (1986). The Mantuan 'Orfeo'. In J. Whenham, ed., *Claudio Monteverdi: Orfeo*. Cambridge, UK: Cambridge University Press, pp. 1–9.

Fortune, N. (2001). *Sprezzatura*. Grove music online. www.oxfordmusiconline.com/subscriber/article/grove/music/26468.

Galilei, V. (1581). *Dialogo di Vincentio Galilei nobile fiorentino della musica antica, et della moderna*. Florence, Italy: Georgio Marescotti.

Garcia, M. (1984). *Traité Complet de l'Art du Chant* (D. V. Paschke, ed. & trans.). New York: Da Capo Press. (Original work published 1847, Paris, France: L'auteur).

Godøy, R. I. (2011). Sound-action awareness in music. In D. I. Clarke & E. F. Clarke, eds., *Music and Consciousness: Philosophical, Psychological, and Cultural Perspectives*. New York: Oxford University Press, pp. 231–243.

Godøy, R. I. (2017). Key-postures, trajectories and sonic shapes. In D. Leech-Wilkinson & H. Prior, eds., *Music and Shape*. New York: Oxford University Press, pp. 4–29.

Goehr, L. (1992). *The Imaginary Museum of Musical Works: An Essay in the Philosophy of Music*. Oxford: Clarendon Press.

Goodman, N. (1976). *Languages of Art: An Approach to a Theory of Symbols*, 2nd ed., Indianapolis, IN: Hackett.

Gordon, B. (2004). *Monteverdi's Unruly Women: The Power of Song in Early Modern Italy*. Cambridge, UK: Cambridge University Press.

Grant, R. M. (2014). *Beating Time and Measuring Music in the Early Modern Era*. Oxford, UK: Oxford University Press.

Grout, D. J., & Williams, H. W. (2003). *A Short History of Opera*, 4th ed. New York: Columbia University Press.

Hanning, B. R. (1980). *Of Poetry and Music's Oower: Humanism and the Creation of Opera*. Ann Arbor, MI: UMI Research Press.

Hanning, B. R. (2011). Monteverdi's three genera: A study in terminology. In R. Wistreich, ed., *Monteverdi*. Aldershot, UK: Ashgate, pp. 265–290.

Haraway, D. (2004). *The Haraway Reader*. New York:Routledge.

Harnoncourt, N. (1988). *Baroque Music Today: Music as Speech: Ways to a New Understanding of Music* (R. G. Pauly, ed., & M. O. Neil, trans.). Portland, OR: Amadeus Press.

Haynes, B. (2007). *The End of Early Music: A Period Performer's History of Music for the Twenty-First Century.* Oxford, UK: Oxford University Press.

Haynes, B., & Burgess, G. (2016). *The Pathetick Musician: Moving an Audience in the Age of Eloquence.* New York: Oxford University Press.

Heller, W. (2003). *Emblems of Eloquence: Opera and Women's Voices in Seventeenth-Century Venice.* Berkeley: University of California Press.

Heller, W. (2014). *Music in the Baroque: Western Music in Context.* New York: Norton.

Higgins, J. (1976). From prince to populace: Patronage as a determinant of change in South Indian (Karnatak) music. *Asian Music, 7*(2), 20–26.

Horodowich, L. (2005). Armchair travelers and the Venetian discovery of the New World. *The Sixteenth Century Journal, 36*(4), 1039–1062.

Hunter, K. (2013). The cognitive body: Using embodied cognition as a tool in performance-making. In S. Reeve, ed., *Body and Performance.* Vol. II of *Ways of Being a Body.* Devon, UK: Triarchy Press, pp. 163–175.

Husserl, E. (2001). *The Idea of Phenomenology* (L. Hardy, trans.). Dordrecht, Netherlands: Kluwer Academic Press. (Original work delivered as lectures in April–May 1907, and published as Ding und Raum: Vorlesungen).

IRENCO – Indian Record Manufacturing Company. (2014, July 22). *G. N. Balasubramaniam: Carnatic – vocal (1910–1965)* [Video file]. https://youtu.be/bgEpgmEitOs?t=21m7s.

Irving, D.R. (2010). *Colonial Counterpoint: Music in Early Modern Manila.* Oxford University Press.

Järviö, P. (2006). The life and world of a singer: Finding my way. *Philosophy of Music Education Review, 14*(1), 65–77.

Järviö, P. (2011). *A singer's sprezzatura – A phenomenological study on speaking in tones of Italian early Baroque music* [online]. Abstract www.academia .edu/592511/A_Singers_Sprezzatura._A_Phenomenological_Study_on_Spe aking_in_Tones_of_Italian_Early_Baroque_Music.

Jayalakshmi, R. S. (2002). Gamakas explained in Sangita-sampradaya-pradarsini of Subbarama Diksitar [Doctoral dissertation]. University of Madras, Chennai, India.

Jaya TV. (2018, January 11). *Margazhi Mahautsavam – Dr. Sudha Raghunathan* [Video file]. https://youtu.be/VDPcn52Wxio?t=8m13s.

Kaleva, D. (2014). Performance research: A performance-led study of *Lamento d'Arianna* with historically informed rhetorical gesture. *Musicology Australia, 36*(2), 209–234.

Kartikeyan, V., Nandakumar, R., & Vishwanath, P. (2018). *Discover the Alchemist Within: Taking the First Step towards Personal Growth*. New Delhi: Sage.

Kassebaum, G. R. (2000). Karnatak raga. In A. Arnold, ed., *South Asia: The Indian Subcontinent*. Vol. V of *The Garland Encyclopedia of World Music*. New York: Garland, pp. 89–109.

Katz, R. (1994). *The Powers of Music: Aesthetic Theory and the Invention of Opera*. New Brunswick, NJ: Transaction.

Kaufmann, W. (1976). *The Rāgas of South India: A Catalouge of Scalar Material*. Bloomington, IN: Indiana University Press.

Komaragiri, M. M. (2011). Synopsis of the Doctoral Dissertation 'Pitch Analysis in Karnātaka Music – An Examination of Intonation and Modern Theories of 22 Śruti-s', University of Madras, Chennai, India [Online document]. www .dropbox.com/s/gyiypy8psk4ug69/AE-MadhuMohanKomaragiri-Pitch-Analysis-in-Karnataka-Music-0443.pdf.

Komaragiri, M. M. (2013). *Pitch Analysis in South Indian music: With a Critical Examination of the Theory of 22 Śrutis*. New Delhi: Munshiram Manoharlal.

Krishna, T. M. (2013). *A Southern Music: The Karnatik Story*. New Dehli: Harper Collins.

Krishna, T. M. (2018). *Reshaping Art*. New Dehli: Aleph.

Krishna, T. M., & Ishwar, V. (2012). Karnatik music: Svara, gamaka, motif and raga identity. In X. Serra, P. Rao, H. Murthy, & B. Bozkurt, eds., *Proceedings of the 2nd CompMusic Workshop*. Istanbul: Universitat Pompeu Fabra, pp. 12–18.

Krishnaswami, S. (2017). *Musical Instruments of India*. New Delhi: Publications Division, Ministry of Information & Broadcasting.

Kurtzman, J. G. (2000). *The Monteverdi Vespers of 1610: Music, Context, Performance*. New York: Oxford University Press.

Lakerveld, M. (Director). (2011, January 9). *Orfeo in India: An adaptation from the opera L'Orfeo by Claudio Monteverdi* [Video File}. www.youtube.com /watch?v=e611w6NpeZ8.

Lawrence-King, A. (2014). Il palpitar del core: The heart-beat of the 'first opera.' In D. Crispin & B. Gilmore, eds., *Artistic Experimentation in Music: An Anthology*. Leuven, Belgium: Leuven University Press, pp. 157–166.

Lawrence-King, A. (2015, January 25). *Play it again, Sam! The truth about Caccini's 'sprezzatura'* [Blog Post]. https://andrewlawrenceking.com/2015/ 01/25/play-it-again-sam-the-truth-about-caccinis-sprezzatura/.

Lawrence-King, A. (2017, August 31). *Emotions in early opera* [Blog Post]. https://andrewlawrenceking.com/2017/08/31/emotions-in-early-opera/.

Leach, E., Fallows, D., & Van Orden, K. (2015). Recent trends in the study of music of the fourteenth, fifteenth, and sixteenth centuries. *Renaissance Quarterly, 68*(1), 187–227.

Leech-Wilkinson, D. (2017). 'Future musicianship and present educational practices': A response to eight questions on the future of the conservatoire as an institution. *Music + Practice, 3.* www.musicandpractice.org/volume-3/leech-wilkinson/.

Leech-Wilkinson, D. & Prior, H. M. (2014). Heuristics for expressive performance. In D. Fabian, R. Timmers & E. Schubert, eds., *Expressiveness in Music Performance: Empirical Approaches across Styles and Cultures.* Oxford, UK: Oxford University Press, pp. 34–58.

Lindenberger, H. (1998). *Opera in History: From Monteverdi to Cage.* Stanford, CA: Stanford University Press.

MacNeil, A. (2003). *Music and Women of the Commedia dell'Arte in the Late Sixteenth Century.* New York: Oxford University Press.

Maffei, G. C. (1979). Letter on singing. In C. C. MacClintock, ed., & trans., *Readings in the History of Music in Performance.* Bloomington: Indiana University Press, pp. 38–60. (Original work published 1562).

Mani, C. (2011, January 28). *Isai Payanam – DVD6 – Hamirkalyani* [Video file]. https://youtu.be/fldteKFHruI.

Mani, C. (2012, April 15). *Inta Saukhya – Kapi* [Video file]. https://youtu.be/WrrOT-oZYZE?t=483.

Mani, C. (2018a, July 31). *Researching ornamentation in Monteverdi's Possente Spirto through reflective practice* [Video file]. https://youtu.be/I2IN8Q7jzXs.

Mani, C. (2018b, April 25). *Monteverdi reimagined: L'Orfeo from a Carnatic perspective* [Video file]. https://youtu.be/9szMfVtHQmQ.

Mani, C. (2019a). *Hybridising Karnatik Music and Early Opera: A journey through voice, word, and gesture* [Doctoral dissertation]. Griffith University, Brisbane, Australia. http://hdl.handle.net/10072/386762. Accessed 20 September 2019.

Mani, C. (2019b). Approaching Italian *gorgie* throughKarnatik *brigha:* An *essai* on intercultural vocal transmission. *Theatre, Dance and Performance Training, 10*(3), 410–417.

Mani, C. (2019c). *Practise, process, and preach: An intercultural embodied approach to understanding ornamentation* [Blog post]. http://theatredanceperformancetraining.org/2019/12/practise-process-and-preach-an-intercultural-embodied-approach-to-understanding-ornamentation/.

Mani, C. (2020a). On breaking with. *Journal of Interdisciplinary Voice Studies* 4(1), 59–80. https://doi.org/10.1386/jivs_00016_1.

Mani, C. (2020b). The Eco-Mesh Approach: A Sustainable Methodology for Socio-Culturally Interrogative Artistic Research. *RUUKKU – Studies in Artistic Research, 14* [Online]. https://doi.org/10.22501/ruu.679814.

McClary, S. K. (1991). *Feminine Endings: Music, Gender, and Sexuality.* Minneapolis: University of Minnesota Press.

McClary, S. K. (2004. *Moral Subjectivities: Self-Fashioning in the Italian Madrigal.* Berkeley: University of California Press.

Merleau-Ponty, M. (1993). Cézanne's doubt. In G. Johnson, ed., & M. B. Smith, trans., *The Merleau-Ponty Aesthetics Reader: Philosophy and Painting.* Evanston, IL: Northwestern University Press, pp. 59–75. (Original work published 1945, Paris, France: Gallimard).

Mersenne, M. (1636). *Harmonie Universelle.* Paris: Cramoisy.

Monteverdi, C. (1615). *L'Orfeo: Favola in Musica* [Score], 2nd edn. Venice, Italy: Ricciardo Amadino. https://imslp.org/wiki/Special:ReverseLookup/30835. (Original work published 1609, Venice, Italy: Ricciardo Amadino).

Monteverdi, C. (1968). *L'Orfeo: Favola in Musica for Soloists, Chorus and Orchestra* [Score] (D. Stevens, ed.). Kent, UK: Novello. (Original work published 1609, Venice, Italy: Ricciardo Amadino).

Monteverdi, C. (1993). *L'Orfeo: Favola in Musica* [Score] (C. Bartlett, ed.). Huntington, UK: King's Music. (Original published 1609, Venice, Italy: Ricciardo Amadino).

Monteverdi, C. (2016). *L'Orfeo: Favola in Music in un Prologo e Cinque Atti* [Score and commentary] (R. Alessandrini, ed.). Kassel, Germany: Bärenreiter. (Original work published 1609, Venice, Italy: Ricciardo Amandino).

Monteverdi Festival. (2017). *The making of a genius: Cláudio Monteverdi from Cremona to Mantua.* International Conference: Pavia University, Cremona & Conservatorio di Musica 'Lucio Campiani' di Mantova, Mantua. www.monteverdifestivalcremona.it/en/450-archive/detail/the-making-of-a-genius-claudio-monteverdi-from-cremona-to-mantua.html.

Monteverdi, C. (Composer) & Gardiner, J. E. (Conductor). (1990). *L'Orfeo* [CD]. Archiv Produktion.

Monteverdi, C. (Composer) & Harnoncourt, N. (Conductor). (1992). *L'Orfeo* [CD]. Teldec Das Alte Werk.

Monteverdi, C. (Composer) & Medlam, C. (Conductor). (1984). Monteverdi's L'Orfeo [CD]. London: EMI.

Monteverdi, C. (Composer) & Savall, J. (Conductor). (2003). *Monteverdi: L'Orfeo* [DVD]. OpusArte.

Monteverdi, C., & Stevens, D. (Trans.) (1980). *The Letters of Claudio Monteverdi.* London, UK: Faber & Faber.

Morris, R., & Ravikiran, C. N. (2006). Ravikiran's concept of melharmony: An inquiry into harmony in south Indian ragas. *Music Theory Spectrum, 28*(2), 255–276.

Mudaliyar, A. M. C. (ed.). (1982). *Oriental music in European notation (Reprint)*. Chennai, India: Cosmo Publications. (Original work published 1893).

Nagley, J., & Bujić, B. (2002). Doctrine of the affections. *Grove music online*. http://oxfordmusiconline.com/subscriber/opr/t114/e95.

Nayak, S. (2000). Review: Women musicians of the Karnatak tradition [Review of the book The Madras quartet: Women in Karnatak music, by I. Menon]. *Indian International Centre Quarterly, 27*(2), 171–174.

Nettl, B. (2009). On learning the Radif and improvisation in Iran. In G. Solis & B. Nettl, eds., *Musical Improvisation: Art, Education, and Society*. Chicago: University of Illinois Press, pp. 185–199.

Newcomb, A. A. (1978). *The Madrigal at Ferrara, 1579–1597*. Princeton, NJ: Princeton University Press.

Ossi, M. (2003). *Divining the Oracle: Monteverdi's Seconda Prattica*. Chicago: University of Chicago Press.

Östersjö, S. (2017). Thinking-through-music: On knowledge production, materiality, emobodiment, and subjectivity in artistic research. In J. Impett, ed., *Artistic Research in Music: Discipline and Resistance: Artists and Research at the Orpheus Institute*. Leuven, Belgium: Leuven University Press, pp. 88–107.

Palisca, C. (1985). The Artusi-Monteverdi controversy. In D. Arnold & N. Fortune, eds., *The New Monteverdi Companion*. London, UK: Faber & Faber, pp. 127–158.

Palisca, C. (1989). *The Florentine Camerata: Documentary Studies and Translations*. New Haven, CT: Yale University Press.

Pearson, L. (2016a). *Gesture in Karnatak music: Pedagogy and musical structure in South India* [Doctoral dissertation]. Durham University, UK.

Pearson, L. (2016b). Coarticulation and gesture: An analysis of melodic movement in South Indian raga performance. *Music Analysis, 35*(3), 280–313.

Pesch, L. (1999). *The Illustrated Companion to South Indian Classical Music*, 2nd ed. New Delhi: Oxford University Press.

Pesch, L. (2016). Unity in diversity, antiquity in contemporary practice? South Indian music reconsidered. In M. Gardner & H. Walsdorf, eds., *Musik – politik – identität*. Göttingen, Germany: Universitätsverlag Göttingen, pp. 199–218.

Peterson, I. V. (Trans.). (1989). *Poems to Śiva: The Hymns of the Tamil Saints*. Princeton, NJ: Princeton Library of Asian Translations.

Pirrotta, N. (1984). Monteverdi's poetic choices. In J. Haar, ed. & trans., *Music and Culture in Italy from the Middle Ages to the Baroque: A Collection of Essays*. Cambridge, MA: Havard University Press, pp. 271–316. (Original work published 1968 as Scelte poetiche di Monteverdi, *Nuova Rivista Musicale Italiana, 2,* 10–42, 226–254).

Pirrotta, N., & Fortune, N. (1954). Temperaments and tendencies in the Florentine Camerata. *The Musical Quarterly, 40*(2), 169–189.

Pirrotta, N., & Povoledo, E. (1982). *Music and Theatre from Poliziano to Monteverdi* (K. Eales, trans.). Cambridge, UK: Cambridge University Press.

Potter, J., & Sorrell, N. (2012). *A History of Singing*. Cambridge, UK: Cambridge University Press.

Powers, H. S. (1958a). The background of the South-Indian raga system [Doctoral dissertation]. Princeton University, Princeton, NJ.

Powers, H. S. (1958b). Mode and raga. *The Musical Quarterly, 44*(4), 448–460.

Powers, K. (2018, November 12). Reaping rewards of period performance. *Early Music America*. www.earlymusicamerica.org/web-articles/reaping-rewards-of-period-performance/?fbclid=IwAR3rxLM7BfTwP8bzcsf12k1c4P7UztFsYCvnP7_NFgQmaTVpwFuaMnjCf9k.

Praetorius, M. (1619). *Syntagma Musicum*. Wittenberg: Johannes Richter

Price, C. (1993). Music, style and society. In C. Price, ed., *The Early Baroque Era: From the Late 16th century to the 1660s*. London, UK: Macmillan Press, pp. 1–22.

Ravikiran, C. N., & Morris, R. (2014). Robert Morris and the concept of melharmony.*Perspectives on New Music, 52*(2), 154–161.

Ringer, M. (2006). *Opera's First Master: The Musical Dramas of Claudio Monteverdi*. Princeton, NJ. Amadeus Press.

Rognoni, F. (2007). *Selva di varii passaggi* (S. M. Honea, trans.). www.uco.edu/cfad/files/music/rognoni-selva.pdf (Original work published 1620, Milan, Italy: Filippo Lamazzo).

Rosand, E. (1991). *Opera in Seventeenth-Century Venice: The Creation of a Genre*. Berkeley: University of California Press.

Rosand, E. (2007). *Monteverdi's Last Operas: A Venetian Trilogy*. Berkeley: University of California Press.

Rosand, E. (2011). Monteverdi's mimetic art: L'incoronazione di Poppea. In R. Wistreich, ed., *Monteverdi*. Aldershot, UK: Ashgate, pp. 135–160.

Rubiés, J. (2007). *Travellers and Cosmographers: Studies in the History of Early Modern Travel and Ethnology*. Aldershot, UK: Ashgate.

Sairam, A (2015, December 13). *Aruna Sairam: Kalinga narthana tillana (Isha Yoga Center 2013)* [Video file]. https://youtu.be/7wyfwel3aOM?t=6m10s.

Sambamoorthy, P. (1964). *South Indian Music*, 7th ed. Madras, India: The Indian Music Publishing House.

Savage, R., & Sansone, M. (1989). 'Il Cargo' and the staging of Early Opera: Four chapters from an anonymous treatise circa 1630. *Early Music*, *17*(4), 495–511.

Schachter, M. L. (2015a). Elements of Karnatak music. *Music Theory Online*, *21* (4). https://mtosmt.org/issues/mto.15.21.4/mto.15.21.4.schachter_supp .html.

Schachter, M. L. (2015b). Structural levels in South Indian Music. *Music Theory Online*, 21 (4). https://mtosmt.org/issues/mto.15.21.4/mto.15.21.4.schachter .php.

Scherzi Musicali. (2014, September 30). *Possente Spirto – Monteverdi | Nicolas Achten, Scherzi Musicali (Recording session)* [Video file]. https://youtu.be /7DqleS5fed4.

Schippers, H. (2007). The guru recontextualized? Perspectives on learning North Indian classical music in shifting environments for professional training. *Asian Music*, *38*(1), 123–138.

Schneider, M. T. (2012). Seeing the empress again: On doubling in L'incoronazione di Poppea. *Cambridge Opera Journal*, *24*(3), 249–291.

Schrade, L. (1950). *Monteverdi: Creator of Modern Music*. New York: Norton.

Schulze, H. (2010). Monteverdi's last operas: A Venetian trilogy. By Ellen Rosand. The Cambridge companion to Monteverdi. Ed. By John Whenham and Richard Wistreich [Review of the books *Monteverdi's Last Operas: A Venetian Trilogy*, by E. Rosand; and *The Cambridge Companion to Monteverdi*, by J. Whenham and R. Wistreich (eds.)]. *Music & Letters*, *91* (1), 102–105.

Schwindt, J. (2014). 'All that glisters': Orpheus's failure as an orator and the academic philosophy of the Accademia degli Invaghiti. *Cambridge Opera Journal*, *26*(3), 239–270.

Seshagopalan, T. N. (1983, December). Point-counterpoint. *Sruti*, 1, 3–35.

Smith, P., & Findlen, P. (2013). *Merchants and Marvels: Commerce, Science, and Art in Early Modern Europe*. New York: Routledge.

Solerti, A. (1904). *Le Origini del Melodrama: Testimonianze dei Contemporanei*. Milan: Fratelli Bocca.

Soneji, D. (2011). *Unfinished Gestures: Devadasis, Memory, and Modernity in South India*. Chicago: University of Chicago Press.

Steinheuer, J. (2007). Orfeo (1607). In J. Whenham & R. Wistreich, eds., *The Cambridge Companion to Monteverdi*. Cambridge, UK: Cambridge University Press, pp. 119–140.

Stevens, D. (1985). Selected letters of Monteverdi translated with commentaries. In D. Arnold & N. Fortune, eds., *The New Monteverdi Companion*. London, UK: Faber & Faber, pp. 15–101.

Strohm, R. (ed.). (2018). *Studies on a Global History of Music: The Balzan Musicology Project*. New York: Routledge.

Strunk, O. (1950). *Source Readings in Music History*. New York: Norton.

Stubbs, S. (1994). *L'armonia sonora:* Continuo orchestration in Monteverdi's Orfeo. *Early Music, 22*(1), 87–98.

Subramaniam, T. R. (1985). GNB, the complete musician. In *G. N. B. Trust Commemorates GNB's 75th Birthday: Souvenir*. Chennai, India: G. N. B. Trust.

Subramanian, L. (2006). *From the Tanjore Court to the Madras Music Academy: A Social History of Music in South India*. New Delhi: Oxford University Press

Subramanian, M. (2002). Analysis of Gamakans of Carnatic music using the computer. *Sangreet Natak, 37*(1), 26–47.

Swift, G. N. (1990). South Indian *'gamaka'* and the violin. *Asian Music, 21*(2), 71–89.

Taruskin, R. 1982. On letting the music speak for itself: Some reflections on musicology and performance. *The Journal of Musicology, 1*(3), 338–349.

Taruskin, R. (1988). The pastness of the present and the presence of the past. In N. Kenyon, ed., *Authenticity and Early music: A Symposium*. New York: Oxford University Press, pp. 137–207.

Taruskin, R. (1995). *Text and Act: Essays on Music and Performance*. New York: Oxford University.

Taruskin, R. (2010). *Music in the Seventeenth and Eighteenth Centuries*. Vol. II of *The Oxford History of Western Music*. New York: Oxford University Press.

Terada, Y. (1996). Effects of nostalgia: The discourse of decline in *Periya Mēlam* music of South India. *Bullettin of the National Museum of Ethnology, 21*(4), 921–939.

Terada, Y. (2000). T. N. Rajarattinam pillai and caste rivalry in South Indian classical music. *Ethnomusicology, 44*(3), 460–490.

Thomaidis, K. (2013a). *The grain of a vocal genre: A comparative approach to the singing pedagogies of EVDC integrative performance practice, Korean Pansori, and the Polish centre for theatre practices 'Gardzienice'* [Doctoral dissertation]. University of London, London, UK. https://ethos.bl.uk /OrderDetails.do?uin=uk.bl.ethos.591058

Thomaidis, K. (2013b). The vocal body. In S. Reeve, ed., *Body and Performance*. Vol. II of *Ways of Being a Body*. Devon, UK: Triarchy Press, pp. 85–98.

Toft, R. (2014). *With Passionate Voice: Re-Creative Singing in Sixteenth-Century England and Italy*. New York: Oxford University Press.

Tomlinson, G. (1981). Madrigal, monody, and Monteverdi's 'via naturale·alla immitatione'. *Journal of the American Musicological Society, 34*(1), 60–108.

Tomlinson, G. (1987). *Monteverdi and the End of the Renaissance*. Berkley: University of California Press.

UniArts Helsinki. (2018). Päivi Järviö. www.uniarts.fi/en/päivi-järviö.

Upton, E. (2012). Concepts of authenticity in early music and popular music communities. *Ethnomusicology Review, 17*. https://ethnomusicologyreview.ucla.edu/journal/volume/17/piece/591.

Vedavalli, R. (2011, April). Vedavali speaks: The art of viruttam singing. *Sruti*, 319, 53–54.

Venkatraman, P. N. (1984, July). GNB and his great new bani. *Sruti*, 7, 22–31.

Vicentino, N. (1996). *Ancient Music Adapted to Modern Practice* (M. R. Maniates, trans.). New Haven, CT: Yale University Press. (Original work published 1555, Rome, Italy: Antonio Barre).

Viswanathan, T. (1977). The analysis of Rāga Alāpana in South Indian music. *Asian Music, 9*(1), 13–71.

Viswanathan, T., & Allen, M. H. (2004). *Music in South India: The Karnātak Concert Tradition and Beyond: Experiencing Music, Expressing Culture*. New York: Oxford University Press.

Wade, B. C. (1979). *Music in India: The Classical Traditions*. Englewood, NJ: Prentice Hall.

Waskul, D. & Vannini, P. (eds.). (2006). *Body/Embodiment: Symbolic Interaction and the Sociology of the Body*. New York: Routledge.

Weidman, A. (2001). Questions of voice: On the subject of 'classical' music in South India [Doctoral dissertation]. Columbia University, New York.

Weidman, A. (2006). *Singing the Classical, Voicing the Modern: The Postcolonial Politics of Music in South India*. Durham, NC: Duke University Press.

Wentz, J. (2010). *The relationship between gesture, affect, and rhythmic freedom in the performance of French tragic opera from Lully to Rameau* [Doctoral dissertation]. Universiteit Leiden, Leiden, Netherlands.

Westerlund, H.M. (2019). The return of moral questions: expanding social epistemology in music education in a time of super-diversity. *Music Education Research, 21*(5), pp. 503–516.

Whitney, K. (2015). Following performance across the research frontier. In M. Doğantan-Dack, ed., *Artistic Practice as Research in Music: Theory, Criticism, Practice*. Farnham, UK: Ashgate, pp. 92–104.

Widdess, R. (1995). *The Rāgas of Early Indian Music: Modes, Melodies, and Musical Notation from the Gupta Period to c. 1250*. Oxford, UK: Clarendon Press.

Wilbourne, E. (2008). La Florinda: The performance of Virginia Ramponi Andreini [Doctoral dissertation]. New York University, New York.

Wilbourne, E. (2016). *Seventeenth-Century Opera and the Sound of the Commedia dell'Arte*. Chicago: University of Chicago Press.

Wilson, N. (2013). *The Art of Re-Enchantment: Making Early Music in the Modern Age*. New York: Oxford University Press.

Wistreich, R. (1994). 'La voce è grata assai, ma . . . ': Monteverdi on singing. *Early Music, 22*(1), 7–20.

Wistreich, R. (2000). Reconstructing pre-Romantic singing technique. In J. Potter, ed., *The Cambridge Companion to Singing*. Cambridge, UK: Cambridge University Press, pp. 178–191.

Wistreich, R. (2007). Monteverdi in performance. In J. Whenham & R. Wistreich, eds., *The Cambridge Companion to Monteverdi*. Cambridge, UK: Cambridge University Press, pp. 261–279.

Wistreich, R. (ed.). (2011). *Monteverdi*. Aldershot, UK: Ashgate.

Wistreich, R. (2012). Vocal performance in the seventheenth century. In C. Lawson & R. Stowell, eds., *The Cambridge History of Musical Performance*. Cambridge, UK: Cambridge University Press, pp. 398–421.

Wistreich, R. (2013). 'Nach der jetzig Newen Italienischen Manier zur guten art im singen sich gewehnen:' The trillo and the migration of Italian noble singing. In S. Ehrmann-Herfort & S. Leopold, eds., *Migration und Identität: Wanderbewegungen und Kulturkontakte in der Musikgeschichte*. Kassel, Germany: Bärenreiter, pp. 138–150.

Wistreich, R. and Potter, J. (2013). Singing early music: A conversation. *Early Music, 41*(1), 22–26.

Zarlino, G. (1968). *The Art of Counterpoint: Part III of 'Le Istitutioni Harmoniche 1558*, (C. Palisca, trans.). New Haven, CT: Yale University Press. (Original work published 1558, Venice, Italy: Zarlino).

Zvelebil, K. V. (1973). *The Smile of Murugan: On Tamil Literature of South India*. New Delhi: Brill.

Acknowledgements

I extend heartfelt gratitude to Professor Stephen Emmerson and Dr Catherine Grant from Queensland Conservatorium Griffith University, my PhD advisors. Huge thanks to the 21st Century Elements Series Editor Professor Simon Zagorski-Thomas for his guidance and insights. Sincere thanks to Professor Richard Wistreich, Royal College of Music, for the rich experiences he shared with me in relation to the pre-romantic voice and its alignments with Indian Classical vocal styles. Many thanks to Dr Jack Walton for the meticulous proofreading. I acknowledge the Griffith University Postgraduate Award for supporting this research.

Cambridge Elements ≡

Elements in Twenty-First Century Music Practice

Simon Zagorski-Thomas
London College of Music, University of West London
Simon Zagorski-Thomas is a Professor at the London College of Music (University of West London, UK) and founded and runs the 21st Century Music Practice Research Network. He is series editor for the Cambridge Elements series and Bloomsbury book series on 21st Century Music Practice. He is ex-chairman and co-founder of the Association for the Study of the Art of Record Production. He is a composer, sound engineer and producer and is, currently, writing a monograph on practical musicology. His books include *Musicology of Record Production* (2014; winner of the 2015 IASPM Book Prize), *The Art of Record Production: an Introductory Reader for a New Academic Field* co-edited with Simon Frith (2012), the *Bloomsbury Handbook of Music Production* co-edited with Andrew Bourbon (2020) and the *Art of Record Production: Creative Practice in the Studio* co-edited with Katia Isakoff, Serge Lacasse and Sophie Stévance (2020).

About the Series

Elements in Twenty-First Century Music Practice has developed out of the 21st Century Music Practice Research Network, which currently has around 250 members in 30 countries and is dedicated to the study of what Christopher Small termed musicking – the process of making and sharing music rather than the output itself. Obviously this exists at the intersection of ethnomusicology, performance studies, and practice pedagogy / practice-led-research in composition, performance, recording, production, musical theatre, music for screen and other forms of multi-media musicking. The generic nature of the term '21st Century Music Practice' reflects the aim of the series to bring together all forms of music into a larger discussion of current practice and to provide a platform for research about any musical tradition or style. It embraces everything from hip-hop to historically informed performance and K-pop to Inuk throat singing.

Cambridge Elements ≡

Elements in Twenty-First Century Music Practice

Printed in the United States
by Baker & Taylor Publisher Services